italian kitchen

Published in 2007 by Murdoch Books Pty Limited.
www.murdochbooks.com.au

Murdoch Books Australia
Pier 8/9, 23 Hickson Road
Millers Point NSW 2000
Phone: + 61 (0) 2 8220 2000
Fax: + 61 (0) 2 8220 2558

Murdoch Books UK Limited
Erico House, 6th Floor
93–99 Upper Richmond Road
Putney, London SW15 2TG
Phone: + 44 (0) 20 8785 5995
Fax: + 44 (0) 20 8785 5985

Chief Executive: Juliet Rogers
Publishing Director: Kay Scarlett

Design Manager: Vivien Valk
Concept & Art Direction: Sarah Odgers
Design: Jacqueline Duncan
Project Manager: Rhiain Hull
Editor: Gordana Trifunovic
Photographer: Jared Fowler
Production: Adele Troeger
Stylist: Cherise Koch
Food preparation: Alan Wilson
Introduction text: Leanne Kitchen
Recipes developed by the Murdoch Books Test Kitchen

National Library of Australia Cataloguing-in-Publication Data
Italian kitchen. Includes index.
ISBN 978 1 74045 968 6 (pbk.) ISBN 1 74045 968 7 (pbk.)
1. Cookery, Italian. I. Trifunovic, Gordana. II. Price, Jane (Jane Paula Wynn). (Series: Kitchen Classics; 4). 641.5945

Printed by 1010 Printing International Ltd. in 2007. PRINTED IN CHINA.

IMPORTANT: Those who might be at risk from the effects of salmonella poisoning (the elderly, pregnant women, young children and those suffering from immune deficiency diseases) should consult their doctor with any concerns about eating raw eggs.

CONVERSION GUIDE: You may find cooking times vary depending on the oven you are using. For fan-forced ovens, as a general rule, set the oven temperature to 20°C (35°F) lower than indicated in the recipe. We have used 20 ml (4 teaspoon) tablespoon measures. If you are using a 15 ml (3 teaspoon) tablespoon, for most recipes the difference will not be noticeable. However, for recipes using baking powder, gelatine, bicarbonate of soda (baking soda), small amounts of flour, add an extra teaspoon for each tablespoon specified.

italian kitchen

THE ITALIAN RECIPES YOU MUST HAVE

SERIES EDITOR **JANE PRICE**

MURDOCH BOOKS

CONTENTS

THE FLAVOURS OF ITALY

The world is full of great, national cuisines but surely none is more loved, nor more universally consumed, than that from Italy. Witness the insinuation into dining rooms the globe over of Italian staples like ravioli and pizza, risotto and lasagne, biscotti, frittata, carpaccio and panna cotta. From Italy comes a wealth of definitive foods and flavours; who doesn't love the green, basil tang of pesto, adore the salty-sweet meatiness of prosciutto or could imagine life without the savoury smack of sun-dried tomatoes, parmesan cheese, salami, capers or anchovies? Perhaps Italian cooking is so popular because it is quietly sophisticated, bursting with flavour and relatively simple to make. Sunny and laid-back like the inhabitants of her shores, the feel-good food of Italy is as worthy of an intimate sit-down dinner party as it is appropriate for a casual feast to be shared by a rowdy mob of famiglia and amici.

Strictly speaking, though, it is a nonsense to talk of 'Italian' food. The respected food writer Claudia Roden goes so far as to exclaim, 'There is no such thing as Italian cooking. Only Sicilian, Piedmontese, Neopolitan, Venetian … and so on'. Italy is fiercely regional in its eating habits. The cookery of the north, traditionally rich in dairy products, meats, polenta and rice, is still quite distinct from that of the south, where tomato-based sauces, pasta, olive oil and fish conventionally hold sway. Whichever part of Italy a recipe or dish hails from though, it is bound to find favour at the table. Italian food never fails to please and, thankfully, isn't subject to the vagaries of faddism and fashion. From the perfect simplicity of chicken liver crostini and stuffed sardines, through to the baroque splendour of Zuccotto, Zuppa Inglese or a Sicilian cheesecake (and all the meat, fish and vegetables in between), no cook's repertoire is complete without an excellent collection of recipes from the beloved cucina italiana.

ANTIPASTO

STUFFED ZUCCHINI FLOWERS

75 g (2¹/₂ oz) plain (all-purpose) flour
100 g (3¹/₂ oz) mozzarella cheese
10 anchovy fillets, halved lengthways
10 basil leaves, torn
20 zucchini (courgette) flowers, stems and pistils removed (see Note)
olive oil, for pan-frying
2 lemon wedges, to serve

MAKES 20

Put the flour in a bowl and add about 250 ml (9 fl oz/1 cup) water — enough to obtain a creamy consistency. Add a pinch of salt and mix well to combine.

Cut the mozzarella into 20 matchsticks. Pat dry the anchovies with paper towels. Insert a piece of mozzarella, half an anchovy fillet and some basil into each zucchini blossom. Press the petals closed.

Pour the oil into a heavy-based frying pan to a depth of 2.5 cm (1 inch). Heat the oil to 180°C (350°F), or until a cube of bread dropped into the oil browns in 15 seconds.

Dip one zucchini flower at a time in the batter, shaking off the excess. Cook in batches for 3 minutes, or until crisp and golden. Drain on paper towels. Season and serve immediately with lemon wedges.

PREPARATION TIME: 20 MINUTES   COOKING TIME: 15 MINUTES

NOTE: Zucchini flowers are available in the male (the flower has a stalk) or female (the flower has a baby zucchini attached) form. They are sold in speciality fruit and vegetable shops. Wash thoroughly before use and make sure there are no insects hidden inside.

TOMATO AND BASIL CROSTINI

4 vine-ripened tomatoes, roughly
chopped
1 handful basil, torn
2 tablespoons extra virgin olive oil
1 baguette, cut into 12 slices
1 large garlic clove

SERVES 4

Preheat the oven to 190°C (375°F/Gas 5). Gently squeeze any excess juice from the tomato, or drain in a sieve. Combine the tomato, basil and oil in a small bowl and season well.

Bake the bread on a baking tray for 2–3 minutes on each side, or until golden. While hot, rub one side of each slice with the garlic, then top with the tomato mixture.

PREPARATION TIME: 10 MINUTES   COOKING TIME: 5 MINUTES

OLIVE CROSTINI

150 g (5¹/₂ oz/1 cup) pitted Kalamata olives
4 anchovy fillets
2 tablespoons baby capers, rinsed and
squeezed dry
1 garlic clove
2 tablespoons chopped basil
60 ml (2 fl oz/¹/₄ cup) olive oil
1 baguette, cut into 12 slices

SERVES 4

Preheat the oven to 190°C (375°F/Gas 5). Combine all the ingredients except the bread in a food processor and process in short bursts until finely chopped but not smooth. Season to taste.

Bake the bread on a baking tray for 2–3 minutes on each side, or until golden. Spread with the paste.

PREPARATION TIME: 10 MINUTES   COOKING TIME: 5 MINUTES

Tomato and basil crostini

FRIED WHITEBAIT

40 g (1¹/₂ oz/¹/₃ cup) plain (all-purpose)
flour
30 g (1 oz/¹/₄ cup) cornflour (cornstarch)
2 teaspoons finely chopped flat-leaf
(Italian) parsley
oil, for deep-frying
500 g (1 lb 2 oz) whitebait
1 lemon, cut into wedges, to serve

SERVES 6

Combine the sifted flours and parsley in a bowl and season.

Fill a deep, heavy-based frying pan one-third full of oil and heat to 180°C (350°F), or until a cube of bread dropped into the oil browns in 15 seconds.

Toss the whitebait in the flour mixture, shake off the excess flour, and deep-fry in batches for 1¹/₂ minutes, or until pale and crisp. Drain well on crumpled paper towels. Serve with lemon wedges.

PREPARATION TIME: 10 MINUTES   COOKING TIME: 10 MINUTES

CARPACCIO

400 g (14 oz) beef eye fillet
1 tablespoon extra virgin olive oil
rocket (arugula) leaves, torn, to serve
60 g (2¼ oz) parmesan cheese, shaved, to serve
black olives, cut into slivers, to serve

SERVES 8

Remove all the visible fat and sinew from the beef, then freeze for 1–2 hours, until firm but not solid. This makes the meat easier to slice thinly.

Cut paper-thin slices of beef with a large, sharp knife. Arrange on a serving platter and allow to return to room temperature.

Just before serving, drizzle with oil, then scatter with rocket, parmesan and olives.

PREPARATION TIME: 15 MINUTES +   COOKING TIME: NIL

NOTE: The beef can be cut into slices a few hours in advance, covered and refrigerated. Drizzle with oil and garnish with the other ingredients just before serving.

CRUMBED ANCHOVIES

800 g (1 lb 12 oz) fresh anchovies
2 eggs
dry breadcrumbs, for coating
150 g (5½ oz) butter
1 lemon, cut into wedges, to serve

SERVES 4

To clean the anchovies, scrape a small knife along the body of each one, starting at the tail end, to remove any scales. This is best done under cold running water. Make a slit along the gut. Cut off the head and pull it away from the body slowly so that the intestines come away with the head. Press open flat on a work surface, press along the backbone with the palm of your hand, then gradually ease out the backbone. Wash the fish briefly and pat dry carefully with paper towels.

Beat the eggs with a little salt in a bowl. Dip the anchovies in the egg mixture, drain off the excess, then coat evenly in the breadcrumbs, pressing on gently.

Melt the butter in a large frying pan and fry the anchovies in batches until golden brown, turning once. Drain on crumpled paper towels. Sprinkle with salt and serve with lemon wedges.

PREPARATION TIME: 20 MINUTES   COOKING TIME: 15 MINUTES

ASPARAGUS AND MINT FRITTATA

6 eggs

35 g (1¹/₄ oz/¹/₃ cup) grated pecorino or parmesan cheese

1 handful mint, finely shredded

200 g (7 oz) baby asparagus spears

2 tablespoons extra virgin olive oil

SERVES 4

Put the eggs in a large bowl, beat well, then stir in the cheese and mint and set aside.

Trim the woody part off the asparagus, then cut the asparagus diagonally into 5 cm (2 inch) pieces. Heat the oil in a 20 cm (8 inch) frying pan. Add the asparagus and cook for 4–5 minutes, until tender and bright green. Season, then reduce the heat to low.

Pour the egg mixture over the asparagus and cook for 8–10 minutes. During cooking, use a spatula to gently pull the sides of the frittata away from the sides of the pan and tip the pan slightly so the egg runs underneath the frittata.

When the mixture is nearly set but still slightly runny on top, place the pan under a grill (broiler) for 1–2 minutes, until the top is set and just browned. Serve warm or at room temperature.

PREPARATION TIME: 10 MINUTES   COOKING TIME: 20 MINUTES

MARINATED EGGPLANT

750 g (1 lb 10 oz) slender eggplant (aubergine)
60 ml (2 fl oz/¼ cup) olive oil, plus extra
2 tablespoons balsamic vinegar
2 garlic cloves, crushed
1 anchovy fillet, finely chopped
2 tablespoons chopped flat-leaf (Italian) parsley

SERVES 6–8

Cut the eggplant into thick diagonal slices. Put in a colander, sprinkle with salt and leave to stand over a bowl for 30 minutes. Rinse under cold water and pat dry with a tea towel (dish towel).

To make the dressing, whisk the oil, vinegar, garlic and anchovy until smooth. Season to taste.

Heat a little oil in a frying pan and brown the eggplant in batches. Transfer to a bowl, toss with the dressing and parsley and marinate for 4 hours. Serve at room temperature.

PREPARATION TIME: 15 MINUTES +   COOKING TIME: 15 MINUTES

SEMI-DRIED TOMATOES

16 roma (plum) tomatoes
3 tablespoons chopped thyme
2 tablespoons olive oil

MAKES 64

Preheat the oven to 160°C (315°F/Gas 2–3). Quarter the tomatoes lengthways and lay, skin side down, on a rack in a baking dish.

Sprinkle with 1 teaspoon each of salt and cracked black pepper and the thyme and roast for 2½ hours. Check occasionally to make sure the tomatoes don't burn.

Toss in the oil and cool before packing into sterilized jars and sealing. Refrigerate for 24 hours before using. Return to room temperature before serving.

PREPARATION TIME: 10 MINUTES +   COOKING TIME: 2 HOURS 30 MINUTES

NOTES: To sterilize storage jars, rinse them thoroughly with boiling water, invert and drain, then place in a very slow oven to dry thoroughly. Don't dry with a tea towel (dish towel).

These tomatoes can be kept in an airtight container in the fridge for up to 7 days.

STUFFED SARDINES

1 kg (2 lb 4 oz) butterflied fresh sardines
60 ml (2 fl oz/¼ cup) olive oil
40 g (1½ oz/½ cup) fresh white
breadcrumbs
30 g (1 oz/¼ cup) sultanas (golden raisins)
40 g (1½ oz/¼ cup) pine nuts, toasted
20 g (¾ oz) tinned anchovy fillets,
drained and mashed
1 tablespoon finely chopped flat-leaf
(Italian) parsley
2 spring onions (scallions), finely chopped

SERVES 4–6

Preheat the oven to 200°C (400°F/Gas 6). Grease a baking dish. Open out each sardine and place, skin side down, on a chopping board.

Heat half the oil in a frying pan. Add the breadcrumbs and cook over medium heat, stirring until light golden. Drain on paper towels.

Put half the fried breadcrumbs in a bowl and stir in the sultanas, pine nuts, anchovies, parsley and spring onion. Season to taste. Spoon about 2 teaspoons of the mixture into each prepared sardine, then carefully fold up to enclose the stuffing.

Place the stuffed sardines in a single layer in the baking dish. Sprinkle any remaining stuffing over the top of the sardines, along with the cooked breadcrumbs. Drizzle with the remaining olive oil and bake for 15–20 minutes.

PREPARATION TIME: 20 MINUTES   COOKING TIME: 25 MINUTES

SAUTÉED BLACK OLIVES

500 g (1 lb 2 oz) wrinkled cured black olives
60 ml (2 fl oz/¼ cup) olive oil
1 onion, sliced
3-4 oregano sprigs

MAKES 500 G (1 LB 2 OZ)

Soak the olives in warm water overnight. Rinse and drain.

Heat the oil in a large frying pan, add the onion and cook over medium heat for 2 minutes. Add the olives and cook for 10 minutes, or until soft.

Remove the olives and onion with a slotted spoon and drain in a colander. Add the oregano, toss and allow to cool completely. Transfer to a sterilized jar. Refrigerate for up to 3 weeks.

PREPARATION TIME: 10 MINUTES +   COOKING TIME: 15 MINUTES

NOTE: To sterilize storage jars, rinse them thoroughly with boiling water, invert and drain, then place in a very slow oven to dry thoroughly. Don't dry with a tea towel (dish towel).

CHILLI GARLIC OLIVES

500 g (1 lb 2 oz) Kalamata olives
zest of 1 orange
1 teaspoon chilli flakes
4 small red chillies, halved
2 garlic cloves, thinly sliced
4 rosemary sprigs
2 tablespoons lemon juice
250 ml (9 fl oz/1 cup) olive oil

MAKES 500 G (1 LB 2 OZ)

Rinse and drain the olives. Make a small incision in the side of each olive. Layer the olives in a sterilized jar with the orange zest, chilli flakes, chillies, garlic and rosemary.

Combine the lemon juice with the olive oil and pour it over the olives. Add extra olive oil to cover, if necessary. Cover and marinate in a cool dark place for 2 weeks.

PREPARATION TIME: 20 MINUTES +   COOKING TIME: NIL

CAPSICUM AND PROSCIUTTO PINWHEELS

1 red capsicum (pepper), seeded,
membrane removed
1 green capsicum (pepper), seeded,
membrane removed
1 yellow capsicum (pepper), seeded,
membrane removed
125 g (4^1/$_2$ oz) cream cheese, softened
25 g (1 oz/^{1}/$_4$ cup) freshly grated parmesan
cheese
2 spring onions (scallions), finely chopped
4 tablespoons chopped oregano
1 tablespoon bottled capers, drained,
squeezed dry and chopped
1 tablespoon pine nuts, chopped
12 thin slices prosciutto

MAKES ABOUT 40

Preheat the grill (broiler). Cut the capsicums into quarters and grill, skin side up, until the skin is black and blistered. Cool in a plastic bag, then peel.

Combine the cream cheese, parmesan, spring onion, oregano, capers and pine nuts in a bowl and mix well.

Lay the prosciutto slices on a work surface, slightly overlapping the edges. Place the capsicum pieces on the prosciutto slices and trim the prosciutto to the same size. Remove the capsicum and spread some cheese mixture on the prosciutto. Top with the capsicum and spread with a little more cheese mixture. Roll up tightly from the short end. Cover and refrigerate for 1 hour, or until firm. Slice into 1 cm (^{1}/$_2$ inch) rounds and serve on toothpicks.

PREPARATION TIME: 30 MINUTES +   COOKING TIME: 10 MINUTES

CALAMARI ROMANA

350 g (12 oz) cleaned small squid tubes
40 g (1½ oz/⅓ cup) plain (all-purpose)
flour
oil, for deep-frying
lemon wedges, to serve

MAKES ABOUT 30

Cut the squid into 1 cm (½ inch) wide rings. Combine the squid rings with ½ teaspoon salt. Cover and refrigerate for about 30 minutes, then dry on crumpled paper towels.

Combine the flour and ¼ teaspoon pepper in a bowl. Fill a deep heavy-based frying pan one-third full of oil and heat to 180°C (350°F), or until a cube of bread dropped into the oil browns in 15 seconds. Toss a few squid rings in the flour mixture, and deep-fry, turning with a long-handled spoon, for 3 minutes, or until lightly browned and crisp. Flour the remaining batches just before frying. Drain on crumpled paper towels and serve hot with the lemon wedges.

PREPARATION TIME: 10 MINUTES +   COOKING TIME: 10 MINUTES

GARLIC AND HERB MARINATED ARTICHOKES

2 garlic cloves, chopped
125 ml (4 fl oz/½ cup) olive oil
2 tablespoons finely chopped dill
15 g (½ oz) finely chopped flat-leaf
(Italian) parsley
2 tablespoons finely chopped basil
2 tablespoons lemon juice
800 g (1 lb 12 oz) tinned artichoke hearts
3 tablespoons finely diced red capsicum
(pepper)

SERVES 8

To make the marinade, combine the garlic, oil, herbs and lemon juice in a bowl and whisk until well combined. Season.

Drain the artichoke hearts and add to the marinade with the red capsicum. Mix well to coat. Cover and marinate in the refrigerator overnight. Return the artichokes to room temperature before serving. Serve as part of an antipasto platter or use in salads.

PREPARATION TIME: 20 MINUTES +   COOKING TIME: NIL

NOTE: The artichokes will keep in an airtight container in the refrigerator for up to a week.

ROASTED BALSAMIC ONIONS

1 kg (2 lb 4 oz) baby onions, unpeeled (see Note)
185 ml (6 fl oz/³/4 cup) balsamic vinegar
2 tablespoons soft brown sugar
185 ml (6 fl oz/³/4 cup) olive oil

SERVES 8

Preheat the oven to 160°C (315°F/Gas 2–3). Bake the onions in a baking dish for 1½ hours. When cool enough to handle, trim the stems from the onions and peel away the skin (the outer part of the root should come away but the onions will remain intact). Add the onions to a 1 litre (35 fl oz/4-cup) sterilized jar.

Combine the vinegar and sugar in a small screw-top jar and stir to dissolve the sugar. Add the oil, seal the jar and shake vigorously until the mixture is combined.

Pour the vinegar mixture over the onions, seal, and turn upside-down to coat. Marinate overnight in the refrigerator, turning occasionally. Return to room temperature and shake to combine the dressing before serving.

PREPARATION TIME: 15 MINUTES +   COOKING TIME: 1 HOUR 30 MINUTES

NOTE: Baby onions, also called pickling or pearl onions, are very small. The ideal size is around 35 g (1¼ oz) each. Sizes will probably range from 20 g (³/4 oz) up to 40 g (1½ oz). The cooking time given is suitable for this range and there is no need to cook the larger ones for any longer. The marinating time given is a minimum time and the onions can be marinated for up to 3 days in the refrigerator. The marinade may separate after a few hours, which is fine — simply stir occasionally.

BEAN AND ROSEMARY DIP

625 g (1 lb 6 oz) tinned butter or
cannellini beans
60 ml (2 fl oz/$\frac{1}{4}$ cup) olive oil
2 garlic cloves, crushed
1 tablespoon finely chopped rosemary
250 ml (9 fl oz/1 cup) chicken or
vegetable stock
2 teaspoons lemon juice

MAKES 2 CUPS

Rinse and drain the beans and set aside. Heat the olive oil in a saucepan and cook the garlic and rosemary for 1 minute, or until the garlic is softened. Add the beans and stock and bring to the boil. Reduce the heat and simmer for 3–4 minutes. Allow to cool.

Blend or process the mixture in batches until smooth. Add the lemon juice and season, to taste. Serve with bread or grissini. This dip can be kept in the refrigerator in a covered container for several days.

PREPARATION TIME: 5 MINUTES   COOKING TIME: 5 MINUTES

GRISSINI

2 teaspoons dried yeast
1 teaspoon sugar
500 g (1 lb 2 oz/4 cups) white strong flour
60 ml (2 fl oz/$\frac{1}{4}$ cup) olive oil
4 tablespoons chopped basil
4 garlic cloves, crushed
50 g (1$\frac{3}{4}$ oz/$\frac{1}{2}$ cup) finely grated
parmesan cheese
2 teaspoons sea salt flakes
2 tablespoons finely grated parmesan
cheese, extra

MAKES 24

Place the yeast, sugar and 310 ml (10$\frac{3}{4}$ fl oz/1$\frac{1}{4}$ cups) warm water in a bowl and stir. Leave in a warm place for 10 minutes, or until bubbles appear on the surface. The mixture should be frothy. If your yeast doesn't foam it is dead, so you will have to discard it and start again.

Sift the flour and 1 teaspoon salt into a bowl and make a well in the centre. Add the yeast mixture and oil and mix to combine. Add more water if the dough is dry. Gather the dough into a ball and turn out onto a lightly floured surface. Knead for 10 minutes, or until soft and elastic. Divide the dough into two portions, add the basil and garlic to one portion, and the parmesan to the other. Knead for a few minutes.

Place each dough in a lightly oiled bowl and cover with plastic wrap. Leave in a warm place for 1 hour, or until doubled in volume. Preheat the oven to 230°C (450°F/Gas 8). Lightly grease two baking trays.

Punch down the doughs and knead each again for 1 minute. Divide each piece of dough into 12 portions, and roll each portion into a stick about 30 cm (12 inches) long and 5 mm ($\frac{1}{4}$ inch) across. Place on the trays and brush with water. Sprinkle the basil and garlic dough with the sea salt flakes, and the cheese dough with the extra parmesan. Bake for 15 minutes, or until crisp and golden brown.

PREPARATION TIME: 40 MINUTES +   COOKING TIME: 15 MINUTES

ARTICHOKE PANZAROTTI

OIL AND WINE DOUGH
250 g (9 oz/2 cups) plain (all-purpose) flour
1/2 teaspoon baking powder
2 teaspoons caster (superfine) sugar
1 egg, lightly beaten
80 ml (2½ fl oz/⅓ cup) olive oil
60 ml (2 fl oz/¼ cup) dry white wine
1 egg, beaten, to glaze

2 tablespoons olive oil
20 g (¾ oz) butter
100 g (3½ oz) lean bacon slices, diced
1 small red onion, sliced
2 garlic cloves, crushed
3 artichoke hearts, finely chopped
2 tablespoons finely chopped flat-leaf (Italian) parsley
150 g (5½ oz) smoked mozzarella cheese, diced
oil, for pan-frying
sea salt, for sprinkling

MAKES 24

Combine the flour, baking powder, sugar and 1/2 teaspoon salt in a bowl. Make a well in the centre, pour in the combined egg, oil and wine and mix with a flat-bladed knife to form a dough. Transfer to a floured surface and gather together into a ball.

Knead for 3–4 minutes, until smooth and elastic. Cover and set aside to rest at room temperature for at least 30 minutes.

Roll the dough out on a floured surface to 3 mm (⅛ inch) thickness. Rest for 10 minutes, then cut out twenty-four 8 cm (3¼ inch) circles. Brush around the edge with beaten egg.

While the dough is resting, heat the oil and butter in a frying pan, then add the bacon, onion, garlic and artichoke. Cook for 10 minutes, adding the parsley for the last 1–2 minutes. Remove from the heat, then drain.

Place 1 teaspoon bacon mixture in the centre of each circle of dough. Add some cheese, and season, to taste. Fold one side of the dough over to meet the other, encasing the filling. Press firmly to seal, then press the edges with a fork. Place on a large plate or baking tray and refrigerate for 30 minutes.

Heat 2 cm (¾ inch) oil in a frying pan to 180°C (350°F), or until a cube of bread dropped into the oil turns golden brown in 15 seconds. Fry the panzarotti, two or three at a time, until puffed and golden on both sides. Remove with a slotted spoon and drain on crumpled paper towels before serving. Sprinkle with sea salt.

PREPARATION TIME: 35 MINUTES +   COOKING TIME: 20 MINUTES

BAKED CAPSICUMS WITH ANCHOVIES

3 yellow capsicums (peppers)
3 red capsicums (peppers)
2 tablespoons extra virgin olive oil
12 anchovy fillets, halved lengthways
3 garlic cloves, thinly sliced
25 g (1 oz) basil, torn
1 tablespoon baby capers, rinsed and squeezed dry
extra virgin olive oil, to serve
sea salt, for sprinkling

SERVES 6

Preheat the oven to 180°C (350°F/Gas 4). Cut each capsicum in half lengthways, leaving the stems intact. If the capsicums are large, quarter them. Remove the seeds and membrane. Drizzle a little of the oil in a baking dish and place the capsicums in, skin side down. Season.

In each capsicum, place a halved anchovy fillet, some garlic and some of the basil. Divide the capers among the capsicums. Season and drizzle with the remaining oil.

Cover the dish with foil and bake the capsicums for 20 minutes. Remove the foil and cook for a further 25–30 minutes, or until the capsicums are tender. Drizzle with a little extra virgin olive oil. Scatter the remaining basil over the capsicums, sprinkle with sea salt and serve warm or at room temperature.

PREPARATION TIME: 15 MINUTES   COOKING TIME: 50 MINUTES

PESTO AND TOMATO TOASTS

PESTO
50 g (1³/₄ oz) basil
50 g (1³/₄ oz/¹/₂ cup) pecans
60 ml (2 fl oz/¹/₄ cup) olive oil
3 garlic cloves

1 baguette, thinly sliced
10 large sun-dried (sun-blushed) tomatoes, cut into thin strips
150 g (5¹/₂ oz) parmesan cheese, thinly shaved

MAKES ABOUT 30

To make the pesto, process the basil leaves, pecans, oil and garlic in a food processor until the mixture is smooth.

Toast the bread slices under a grill (broiler) until brown on both sides.

Spread the pesto evenly over the pieces of toast. Top each slice with sun-dried tomatoes and some of the parmesan.

PREPARATION TIME: 15 MINUTES   COOKING TIME: 5 MINUTES

NOTE: The pesto can be made several days ahead and stored in a jar. Pour a thin layer of olive oil over the top of the pesto to just cover. Pesto can also be frozen in ice cube trays and thawed when required.

ASPARAGUS AND PROSCIUTTO ROLLS

12 prosciutto slices
24 asparagus spears
100 g (3$\frac{1}{2}$ oz) butter, melted
60 g (2$\frac{1}{4}$ oz) parmesan cheese, grated
freshly grated nutmeg
1 lemon

MAKES 24

Preheat the oven to 180°C (350°F/Gas 4). Cut each slice of prosciutto in half lengthways. Cut off the base of each asparagus stem so that the spear is about 9 cm (3$\frac{1}{2}$ inches) long. Bring a saucepan of lightly salted water to the boil, add the asparagus and cook for 1 minute, or until just tender.

Drain the asparagus and pat dry. Brush with the melted butter, then roll the spears in the parmesan. Wrap each asparagus spear in half a slice of prosciutto.

Brush an ovenproof dish, large enough to hold the asparagus in a single layer, with melted butter. Place the asparagus bundles in the dish. Sprinkle with any remaining parmesan, grated nutmeg and cracked black pepper, to taste. Bake for 7 minutes. Squeeze a little fresh lemon juice over the top and serve.

PREPARATION TIME: 20 MINUTES   COOKING TIME: 10 MINUTES

NOTE: Thinly sliced bacon can be substituted for the prosciutto. The rolls can be assembled up to 6 hours ahead, covered and refrigerated. Cook just before serving.

HERB BAKED RICOTTA

1 kg (2 lb 4 oz) wedge full-fat ricotta cheese (see Note)
2 tablespoons thyme
2 tablespoons chopped rosemary
2 tablespoons chopped oregano
15 g (1/2 oz) chopped flat-leaf (Italian) parsley
15 g (1/2 oz) snipped chives
2 garlic cloves, crushed
125 ml (4 fl oz/1/2 cup) olive oil

SERVES 6–8

Pat the ricotta dry with paper towels and place in a baking dish.

Mix the herbs, garlic, oil and 2 teaspoons cracked pepper in a bowl. Spoon onto the ricotta, pressing with the back of a spoon. Cover and refrigerate overnight.

Preheat the oven to 180°C (350°F/Gas 4). Bake for 30 minutes, or until the ricotta is golden. Serve with crusty bread.

PREPARATION TIME: 25 MINUTES +   COOKING TIME: 30 MINUTES

NOTE: If you can't buy a wedge of ricotta, drain the wet ricotta in a colander overnight over a large bowl. Spread half the herb mixture in a 1.25 litre (44 fl oz/5-cup) loaf tin, then spoon the ricotta in and spread with the remaining herbs before baking.

BOCCONCINI TOMATO SKEWERS

20 cherry bocconcini (fresh baby mozzarella cheese) or ovolini
2 tablespoons olive oil
2 tablespoons chopped flat-leaf (Italian) parsley
1 tablespoon snipped chives
20 small cherry tomatoes
40 small basil leaves

MAKES 20

Put the bocconcini in a bowl with the oil, parsley, chives, 1/4 teaspoon salt and 1/2 teaspoon ground black pepper. Cover and refrigerate for at least 1 hour, or preferably overnight.

Cut each cherry tomato in half and thread one half on a skewer or toothpick, followed by a basil leaf, then bocconcini, another basil leaf and then another tomato half. Repeat with more skewers and the remaining ingredients and serve.

PREPARATION TIME: 20 MINUTES +   COOKING TIME: NIL

NOTE: These can be served immediately, or covered and chilled for up to 8 hours.

TUNA AND CANNELLINI BEAN SALAD

400 g (14 oz) tuna steaks
1 tablespoon olive oil
1 small red onion, thinly sliced
1 ripe tomato, seeded and chopped
1 small red capsicum (pepper), seeded
and membrane removed, thinly sliced
800 g (1 lb 12 oz) tinned cannellini beans
2 garlic cloves, crushed
1 teaspoon chopped thyme
4 tablespoons chopped flat-leaf (Italian)
parsley
1½ tablespoons lemon juice
80 ml (2½ fl oz/⅓ cup) extra virgin olive
oil
1 teaspoon honey
100 g (3½ oz) rocket (arugula)
1 teaspoon grated lemon zest

SERVES 4–6

Preheat a barbecue grill plate or flat plate to medium. Place the tuna steaks on a plate, brush with the oil and sprinkle with cracked black pepper on both sides.

Combine the onion, tomato and red pepper in a large bowl. Rinse the cannellini beans under cold running water for 30 seconds, drain and add to the bowl with the garlic, thyme and 3 tablespoons of the parsley.

Place the lemon juice, oil and honey in a small saucepan, bring to the boil, then reduce the heat to low and simmer, stirring, for 1 minute, or until the honey dissolves. Remove from the heat.

Sear the tuna for 1 minute on each side. The meat should still be pink in the middle. Slice into 3 cm (1¼ inch) cubes and combine with the salad. Pour on the warm dressing and toss well.

Place the rocket on a large platter. Top with the salad, season and garnish with the lemon zest and remaining parsley. Serve immediately.

PREPARATION TIME: 25 MINUTES   COOKING TIME: 5 MINUTES

NOTE: Tinned tuna is a delicious substitute for the fresh tuna in this recipe. Drain well before using.

PESTO-TOPPED CHERRY TOMATOES

60 g (2¼ oz) flat-leaf (Italian) parsley, chopped

2 garlic cloves, roughly chopped

2 tablespoons pine nuts, toasted

60 ml (2 fl oz/¼ cup) olive oil

60 g (2¼ oz) freshly grated parmesan cheese

1 handful basil

15 g (½ oz) butter, at room temperature

500 g (1 lb 2 oz) cherry tomatoes

MAKES ABOUT 50

Put the parsley, garlic, pine nuts and oil in a food processor and process. Add the parmesan, basil leaves, butter and freshly ground pepper and process until well combined.

Slice the tops from the cherry tomatoes. Spoon a little mound of the pesto mixture onto the top of each tomato.

PREPARATION TIME: 35 MINUTES   COOKING TIME: NIL

NOTE: The pesto can be made several days ahead. Spoon into a container and cover the surface of the pesto with a thin layer of olive oil. Cover with a lid.

ROSEMARY AND CHEESE BISCUITS

125 g (4½ oz/1 cup) plain (all-purpose) flour

100 g (3½ oz) butter, chopped

1 tablespoon sour cream

60 g (2¼ oz) grated cheddar cheese

60 g (2¼ oz) freshly grated parmesan cheese

3 teaspoons chopped rosemary

3 teaspoons snipped chives

MAKES ABOUT 50

Preheat the oven to 180°C (350°F/Gas 4). Lightly grease two baking trays. Sift the flour and some salt and cracked black pepper into a bowl and add the chopped butter. Rub the butter into the flour with your fingertips until the mixture resembles fine breadcrumbs.

Add the sour cream, cheeses and herbs and mix with a flat-bladed knife. Press the mixture together with your fingers until it forms a soft dough. Press into a ball, wrap in plastic wrap and refrigerate for 15 minutes.

Roll level teaspoons of the mixture into balls and place on the prepared trays, leaving a little room between the biscuits for spreading. Flatten slightly with a lightly floured fork.

Bake for 15–20 minutes, or until lightly golden. Transfer to a wire rack to cool.

PREPARATION TIME: 10 MINUTES +   COOKING TIME: 20 MINUTES

Pesto-topped cherry tomatoes

FRIED STUFFED OLIVES

1 tablespoon olive oil

100 g (3¹/₂ oz) minced (ground) pork and veal

60 g (2¹/₄ oz) pancetta, chopped

3 garlic cloves, crushed

2 teaspoons chopped flat-leaf (Italian) parsley

pinch cayenne pepper

125 ml (4 fl oz/¹/₂ cup) dry white wine

500 ml (17 fl oz/2 cups) chicken stock

25 g (1 oz/¹/₃ cup) fresh white breadcrumbs

1 egg yolk

2 tablespoons grated provolone cheese

1 kg (2 lb 4 oz) large green olives, such as Gordal, pitted

60 g (2¹/₄ oz/¹/₂ cup) plain (all-purpose) flour

1 egg, beaten

100 g (3¹/₂ oz/1 cup) dry breadcrumbs

oil, for deep-frying

SERVES 6–8

Heat the oil in a frying pan over low heat and add the pork and veal, pancetta, garlic and parsley. Cook, stirring, until the pork changes colour. Add the cayenne and season. Increase the heat to high, pour in the wine and cook until almost evaporated. Add the stock, reduce the heat and simmer for 45 minutes, by which time the liquid should have evaporated. If not, increase the heat and reduce it until dry.

Pass the meat mixture through a fine mincer, or process in a food processor until as smooth as possible. Stir in the breadcrumbs, egg yolk and provolone. Using a pastry bag fitted with a small round nozzle, pipe the filling into the olives. Roll in the flour and shake off any excess. Roll in the beaten egg, then the breadcrumbs.

Fill a deep heavy-based saucepan one-third full of oil and heat to 180°C (350°F), or until a cube of bread dropped into the oil browns in 15 seconds. Fry the olives in batches until golden. Drain on paper towels before serving.

PREPARATION TIME: 45 MINUTES   COOKING TIME: 1 HOUR 15 MINUTES

PESTO BOCCONCINI BALLS

3 large handfuls basil
40 g (1¹/2 oz/¹/4 cup) pine nuts
35 g (1¹/4 oz/¹/3 cup) freshly grated
parmesan cheese
2 garlic cloves
80 ml (2¹/2 fl oz/¹/3 cup) olive oil
300 g (10¹/2 oz) bocconcini (fresh baby
mozzarella cheese)

SERVES 4–6

Blend the basil leaves, pine nuts, parmesan and garlic in a food processor until finely chopped. With the motor running, gradually add the olive oil and process until a paste is formed. Transfer the pesto to a bowl and add the bocconcini. Mix very gently, cover and marinate in the refrigerator for 2 hours.

PREPARATION TIME: 10 MINUTES +   COOKING TIME: NIL

NAPOLETANA CROSTINI

100g (3¹/2 oz) unsalted butter, softened
1 baguette, cut into 12 slices
6 bocconcini (fresh baby mozzarella
cheese), quartered
12 anchovy fillets, halved lengthways
2 vine-ripened tomatoes, peeled, cut into
wedges and seeded
1 teaspoon dried oregano

SERVES 4

Preheat the oven to 180°C (350°F/Gas 4). Lightly grease a baking tray.

Butter each bread slice thickly on one side only and top each with two slices of bocconcini. Lay two anchovy halves and a piece of tomato over the cheese on each. Season with oregano, salt and freshly ground pepper and bake for 12–15 minutes.

PREPARATION TIME: 10 MINUTES   COOKING TIME: 15 MINUTES

Pesto bocconcini balls

CHICKEN LIVER CROSTINI

1 baguette, cut into 12 slices
80 ml (2½ fl oz/⅓ cup) extra virgin olive oil
220 g (7¾ oz) chicken livers, trimmed
2 button mushrooms, sliced
4 sage leaves
2 garlic cloves, crushed
pinch ground nutmeg
125 ml (4 fl oz/½ cup) Madeira
1 anchovy fillet
2 teaspoons capers, rinsed and squeezed dry
1 egg yolk

SERVES 4

Preheat the oven to 190°C (375°F/Gas 5). Use half the oil to brush both sides of the bread. Bake on a baking tray for 2–3 minutes on each side, or until golden. Cool.

Heat the remaining oil in a heavy-based frying pan and add the livers, mushrooms and sage. Cook for 5 minutes, stirring often, or until the livers change colour. Add the garlic and nutmeg and season. Cook for 1 minute, add the Madeira and cook until it has evaporated. Transfer to a food processor. Add the anchovy and capers and process until smooth. Add the egg yolk, blend, then taste for seasoning. Spread on the toasts.

PREPARATION TIME: 15 MINUTES   COOKING TIME: 20 MINUTES

PASTA AND RICE

HERB-FILLED RAVIOLI WITH SAGE BUTTER

PASTA
300 g (10½ oz) plain (all-purpose) flour
3 eggs, beaten
60 ml (2 fl oz/¼ cup) olive oil

250 g (9 oz/1 cup) ricotta cheese
2 tablespoons freshly grated parmesan cheese, plus extra, shaved, to garnish
2 teaspoons snipped chives
1 tablespoon chopped flat-leaf (Italian) parsley
2 teaspoons chopped basil
1 teaspoon chopped thyme

SAGE BUTTER
200 g (7 oz) butter
12 sage leaves

SERVES 4

Sift the flour into a bowl and make a well in the centre. Gradually mix in the eggs and oil. Turn out onto a lightly floured surface and knead for 6 minutes, or until smooth. Cover with plastic wrap and leave for 30 minutes.

Mix together the ricotta, parmesan and herbs. Season.

Divide the dough into four even portions. Lightly flour a large work surface and using a floured long rolling pin, roll out one portion from the centre to the edge. Continue, always rolling from in front of you outwards. Rotate the dough often. Fold the dough in half and roll it out again. Continue this process seven times to make a smooth circle of pasta about 5 mm (¼ inch) thick. Roll this sheet out quickly and smoothly to a thickness of 2.5 mm (⅛ inch). Make four sheets of pasta, two slightly larger than the others. Cover with a tea towel (dish towel).

Spread one of the smaller sheets out on a work surface and place heaped teaspoons of filling at 5 cm (2 inch) intervals. Brush a little water between the filling along the cutting lines. Place a larger sheet on top and firmly press the sheets together along the cutting lines. Cut the ravioli with a pastry wheel or knife and transfer to a lightly floured baking tray. Repeat with the remaining dough and filling.

To make the sage butter, melt the butter over low heat in a small heavy-based saucepan, without stirring or shaking. Carefully pour the clear butter into another container and discard the remaining white sediment. Return the clarified butter to a clean pan and heat gently over medium heat. Add the sage leaves and cook until crisp but not brown. Remove and drain on paper towels. Reserve the warm butter.

Cook the ravioli in batches in a large saucepan of salted simmering water for 5–6 minutes, or until tender. Top with warm sage butter and leaves and garnish with shaved parmesan.

PREPARATION TIME: 1 HOUR +   COOKING TIME: 10 MINUTES

NOTE: Don't cook the ravioli in rapidly boiling water or the squares will split and lose the filling.

PENNE ALLA NAPOLITANA

2 tablespoons olive oil
1 onion, finely chopped
2–3 garlic cloves, finely chopped
1 small carrot, finely diced
1 celery stalk, finely diced
800 g (1 lb 12 oz) tinned peeled, chopped tomatoes or 1 kg (2 lb 4 oz) ripe tomatoes, peeled and chopped
1 tablespoon tomato paste (concentrated purée)
3 tablespoons shredded basil
500 g (1 lb 2 oz) penne
freshly grated parmesan cheese, to serve (optional)

SERVES 4–6

Heat the oil in a large frying pan. Add the onion and garlic and cook for 2 minutes, or until golden. Add the carrot and celery and cook for a further 2 minutes.

Add the tomato and tomato paste. Simmer for 20 minutes, or until the sauce thickens, stirring occasionally. Stir in the shredded basil and season to taste.

While the sauce is cooking, cook the pasta in a large saucepan of rapidly boiling salted water until *al dente*. Drain well and return to the pan. Add the sauce to the pasta and mix well. Serve with freshly grated parmesan cheese, if desired.

PREPARATION TIME: 20 MINUTES   COOKING TIME: 25 MINUTES

SPAGHETTI PUTTANESCA

80 ml (2½ fl oz/⅓ cup) olive oil
2 onions, finely chopped
3 garlic cloves, finely chopped
½ teaspoon chilli flakes
6 large ripe tomatoes, diced
4 tablespoons capers, rinsed and squeezed dry
8 anchovy fillets in oil, drained and chopped
150 g (5½ oz) Kalamata olives
3 tablespoons chopped flat-leaf (Italian) parsley
375 g (13 oz) spaghetti

SERVES 6

Heat the olive oil in a saucepan, add the onion and cook over medium heat for 5 minutes. Add the garlic and chilli flakes to the saucepan and cook for 30 seconds. Add the tomato, capers and anchovies. Simmer over low heat for 10–15 minutes, or until the sauce is thick and pulpy. Stir the olives and parsley through the sauce.

While the sauce is cooking, cook the spaghetti in a large saucepan of rapidly boiling salted water until *al dente*. Drain and return to the pan.

Add the sauce to the pasta and stir it through. Season to taste and serve immediately.

PREPARATION TIME: 15 MINUTES   COOKING TIME: 20 MINUTES

ARANCINI

large pinch saffron threads
250 ml (9 fl oz/1 cup) dry white wine
750 ml (26 fl oz/3 cups) chicken stock
100 g (3^1/$_2$ oz) butter
1 onion, finely chopped
1 large garlic clove, crushed
2 tablespoons thyme
220 g (7^3/$_4$ oz/1 cup) risotto rice
50 g (1^3/$_4$ oz/^{1}/$_2$ cup) freshly grated
parmesan cheese
100 g (3^1/$_2$ oz) fresh mozzarella or fontina
cheese, cubed
70 g (2^1/$_2$ oz) dry breadcrumbs
oil, for deep-frying

MAKES 20

Soak the saffron in the wine while you prepare the risotto. Pour the stock into a saucepan and bring to the boil. Reduce the heat, cover with a lid and keep at a low simmer.

Melt the butter in a large saucepan. Cook the onion and garlic over low heat for 3–4 minutes, or until softened but not browned. Add the thyme and rice to the onion and cook, stirring, for 1 minute, or until the rice is well coated. Add the wine and saffron and stir until the wine is all absorbed. Add 125 ml (4 fl oz/^{1}/$_2$ cup) of the hot stock and stir constantly over medium heat until all the liquid is absorbed. Continue adding more stock, 125 ml (4 fl oz/^{1}/$_2$ cup) at a time until all the liquid is absorbed and the rice is tender and creamy; this will take around 25–30 minutes. When making arancini, it is not so essential to keep the rice *al dente* — if it is a little more glutinous, it will stick together better.

Remove the pan from the heat and stir in the parmesan, then spread the mixture out onto a tray covered with plastic wrap. Leave to cool and, for the best results, leave in the fridge to firm up overnight.

To make the arancini, roll a small amount of risotto into a walnut-sized ball. Press a hole in the middle with your thumb, push a small piece of mozzarella or fontina cheese inside and press the risotto around it to enclose in a ball. Repeat with the rest of the risotto. Roll each ball in the breadcrumbs, pressing down to coat well.

Heat enough oil in a deep-fryer or large heavy-based saucepan to fully cover the arancini. Heat the oil to 180°C (350°F), or until a cube of bread dropped into the oil browns in 15 seconds. Cook the arancini in batches, without crowding, for 3–4 minutes. Drain on crumpled paper towels and leave for a couple of minutes before eating. Serve either hot or at room temperature.

PREPARATION TIME: 25 MINUTES +   COOKING TIME: 50 MINUTES

NOTE: Arancini means 'little oranges' and these rice balls are a speciality of Sicily. Traditionally, saffron risotto is used as a basis for arancini. If you can find it, use vialone nano or another riso semifino.

SPAGHETTI CARBONARA

500 g (1 lb 2 oz) spaghetti
8 bacon slices
4 eggs
50 g (1¾ oz/½ cup) freshly grated parmesan cheese
310 ml (10¾ fl oz/1¼ cups) pouring (whipping) cream
snipped chives, to garnish

SERVES 6

Cook the spaghetti in a large saucepan of rapidly boiling salted water until *al dente*. Drain and return to the pan.

While the pasta is cooking, discard the bacon rind and cut the bacon into thin strips. Cook in a heavy-based frying pan over medium heat until crisp. Remove and drain on paper towels.

Beat the eggs, parmesan and cream in a bowl until well combined. Add the bacon and pour the sauce over the warm pasta. Toss gently until pasta is well coated.

Return the pan to the heat and cook over low heat for 1 minute, or until slightly thickened. Season with freshly ground black pepper and serve garnished with snipped chives.

PREPARATION TIME: 10 MINUTES   COOKING TIME: 20 MINUTES

FETTUCINE ALFREDO

500 g (1 lb 2 oz) fettucine or tagliatelle
90 g (3¼ oz) butter
150 g (5½ oz/1½ cups) freshly grated parmesan cheese
310 ml (10¾ fl oz/1¼ cups) pouring (whipping) cream
3 tablespoons chopped flat-leaf (Italian) parsley

SERVES 6

Cook the pasta in a large saucepan of rapidly boiling salted water until *al dente*. Drain and return to the pan.

Meanwhile, heat the butter in a saucepan over low heat. Add the parmesan and cream and bring to the boil, stirring constantly. Reduce the heat and simmer for 10 minutes, or until the sauce has thickened slightly. Add the parsley, and season to taste, and stir well to combine. Add the sauce to the warm pasta and toss well to combine.

PREPARATION TIME: 10 MINUTES   COOKING TIME: 15 MINUTES

CLASSIC LASAGNE

2 tablespoons oil
30 g (1 oz) butter
1 large onion, finely chopped
1 carrot, finely chopped
1 celery stalk, finely chopped
500 g (1 lb 2 oz) minced (ground) beef
150 g (5½ oz) chicken livers, finely chopped
250 ml (9 fl oz/1 cup) tomato passata (puréed tomatoes)
250 ml (9 fl oz/1 cup) red wine
2 tablespoons chopped flat-leaf (Italian) parsley
375 g (13 oz) fresh lasagne sheets
100 g (3½ oz/1 cup) freshly grated parmesan cheese

BÉCHAMEL SAUCE
60 g (2¼ oz) butter
40 g (1½ oz/⅓ cup) plain (all-purpose) flour
560 ml (19¼ fl oz/2¼ cups) milk
½ teaspoon freshly grated nutmeg

SERVES 8

Heat the oil and butter in a heavy-based frying pan and cook the onion, carrot and celery over medium heat until softened, stirring constantly. Increase the heat, add the beef and brown well, breaking up any lumps with a fork. Add the chicken livers and cook until they change colour. Add the tomato passata, wine, parsley, and season to taste. Bring to the boil, reduce the heat and simmer for 45 minutes, then set aside.

To make the béchamel sauce, melt the butter in a saucepan over low heat. Add the flour and stir for 1 minute. Remove from the heat and gradually stir in the milk. Return to the heat and stir constantly until the sauce boils and begins to thicken. Simmer for another minute. Add the nutmeg and season to taste. Place a piece of plastic wrap on the surface of the sauce to prevent a skin forming, and set aside.

Cut the lasagne sheets to fit into a deep, rectangular ovenproof dish.

To assemble, preheat the oven to 180°C (350°F/Gas 4). Grease the ovenproof dish. Spread a thin layer of the meat sauce over the base and follow with a thin layer of béchamel. If the béchamel has cooled and become too thick, warm it gently to make spreading easier. Lay the lasagne sheets on top, gently pressing to push out any air. Continue the layers, finishing with the béchamel. Sprinkle with parmesan and bake for 35–40 minutes, or until golden brown. Cool for 15 minutes before cutting.

PREPARATION TIME: 40 MINUTES   COOKING TIME: 1 HOUR 40 MINUTES

NOTE: Instant lasagne can be used instead of fresh. Follow the manufacturer's instructions. If you prefer, you can leave out the chicken livers and increase the amount of mince.

MUSHROOM RISOTTO

20 g (³/₄ oz) dried porcini mushrooms
1 litre (35 fl oz/4 cups) chicken or
vegetable stock
2 tablespoons olive oil
100 g (3¹/₂ oz) butter, chopped
650 g (1 lb 7 oz) small cap or Swiss brown
mushrooms, stems trimmed, sliced
3 garlic cloves, crushed
80 ml (2¹/₂ fl oz/¹/₃ cup) dry white
vermouth
1 onion, finely chopped
440 g (15¹/₂ oz/2 cups) risotto rice
150 g (5¹/₂ oz/1¹/₂ cups) freshly grated
parmesan cheese

SERVES 4–6

Soak the porcini mushrooms in 500 ml (17 fl oz/2 cups) warm water for 30 minutes. Drain, retaining the liquid. Chop, then pour the liquid through a fine sieve lined with a paper towel.

Put the stock and the mushroom liquid together in a saucepan. Bring to the boil, then reduce the heat, cover and keep at a low simmer.

Heat half the oil and 40 g (1¹/₂ oz) of the butter in a frying pan over high heat. Add all the mushrooms and the garlic to the pan. Cook, stirring, for 10 minutes, or until soft. Reduce the heat to low and cook for a further 5 minutes. Increase the heat, add the vermouth and cook for 2–3 minutes, until evaporated. Set aside.

Heat the remaining olive oil and 20 g (³/₄ oz) butter in a saucepan. Add the onion and cook for 10 minutes, or until soft. Add the rice and stir for 1–2 minutes, or until coated. Add 125 ml (4 fl oz/¹/₂ cup) stock to the pan and stir constantly over medium heat until all the liquid is absorbed. Continue adding more stock, 125 ml (4 fl oz/¹/₂ cup) at a time, stirring, for 20–25 minutes, or until tender. Remove from the heat and stir in the mushrooms, parmesan and the remaining butter. Season to taste.

PREPARATION TIME: 10 MINUTES +   COOKING TIME: 1 HOUR

RISOTTO MILANESE

200 ml (7 fl oz) dry white vermouth or
white wine
large pinch saffron threads
1.5 litres (52 fl oz/6 cups) chicken stock
100 g (3¹/₂ oz) butter
70 g (2¹/₂ oz) beef marrow
1 large onion, finely chopped
1 garlic clove, crushed
360 g (12³/₄ oz/1²/₃ cups) risotto rice
50 g (1³/₄ oz/¹/₂ cup) freshly grated
parmesan cheese

SERVES 6 AS A SIDE DISH

Put the vermouth in a bowl, add the saffron and leave to soak. Pour the stock into a saucepan and bring to the boil. Reduce the heat, cover with a lid and keep at a low simmer.

Melt the butter and beef marrow in a saucepan. Cook the onion and garlic until softened. Stir until well combined. Add the vermouth and saffron to the rice and stir until the liquid has been absorbed. Add 125 ml (4 fl oz/¹/₂ cup) of the hot stock and stir over medium heat until all the liquid is absorbed. Continue adding more stock, 125 ml (4 fl oz/¹/₂ cup) at a time until all the liquid is absorbed and the rice is creamy, this will take around 25–30 minutes. Remove from the heat and stir in the parmesan.

PREPARATION TIME: 20 MINUTES   COOKING TIME: 35 MINUTES

GNOCCHI ROMANA

750 ml (26 fl oz/3 cups) milk
½ teaspoon freshly grated nutmeg
85 g (3 oz/²/3 cup) semolina
1 egg, beaten
150 g (5½ oz/1½ cups) freshly grated
parmesan cheese
60 g (2¼ oz) butter, melted
125 ml (4 fl oz/½ cup) pouring (whipping)
cream
70 g (2½ oz/½ cup) freshly grated
mozzarella cheese

SERVES 4

Line a deep Swiss roll tin (jelly roll tin) with baking paper. Combine the milk and half the nutmeg in a saucepan and season to taste. Bring to the boil, reduce the heat and gradually stir in the semolina. Cook, stirring occasionally, for 5–10 minutes, or until the semolina is very stiff.

Remove the pan from the heat, add the egg and 100 g (3½ oz/1 cup) of the parmesan. Stir to combine and then spread the mixture in the prepared tin. Refrigerate for 1 hour, or until the mixture is firm.

Preheat the oven to 180°C (350°F/Gas 4). Lightly grease a shallow casserole dish. Cut the semolina into rounds using a floured 4 cm (1½ inch) cutter and arrange in the dish.

Pour the melted butter over the top, followed by the cream. Combine the remaining grated parmesan with the mozzarella cheese and sprinkle them on the rounds. Sprinkle with the remaining nutmeg. Bake for 20–25 minutes, or until the mixture is golden.

PREPARATION TIME: 20 MINUTES +   COOKING TIME: 40 MINUTES

ORECCHIETTE WITH BROCCOLI

750 g (1 lb 10 oz) broccoli, cut into florets
450 g (1 lb) orecchiette
60 ml (2 fl oz/¼ cup) extra virgin olive oil
8 anchovy fillets
½ teaspoon chilli flakes
30 g (1 oz/⅓ cup) grated pecorino or parmesan cheese

SERVES 6

Blanch the broccoli in a large saucepan of boiling salted water for 5 minutes, or until just tender. Remove with a slotted spoon, drain well and return the water to the boil. Cook the pasta in the boiling water until *al dente*, then drain well and return to the pan.

Meanwhile, heat the oil in a heavy-based frying pan and cook the anchovies over very low heat for 1 minute. Add the chilli flakes and broccoli. Increase the heat to medium and cook, stirring, for 5 minutes, or until the broccoli is well-coated and beginning to break apart. Season. Add to the pasta, add the cheese and toss.

PREPARATION TIME: 5 MINUTES   COOKING TIME: 15 MINUTES

SPAGHETTI WITH CREAMY LEMON SAUCE

500 g (1 lb 2 oz) spaghetti
250 ml (9 fl oz/1 cup) pouring (whipping) cream
185 ml (6 fl oz/¾ cup) chicken stock
1 tablespoon finely grated lemon zest, plus extra, shredded, to garnish
2 tablespoons finely chopped flat-leaf (Italian) parsley
2 tablespoons snipped chives

SERVES 4

Cook the spaghetti in a large saucepan of rapidly boiling salted water until *al dente*. Drain and return to the pan.

While the spaghetti is cooking, combine the cream, chicken stock and lemon zest in a saucepan over medium heat. Bring to the boil, stirring occasionally. Reduce the heat and simmer gently for 10 minutes, or until the sauce is reduced and thickened slightly.

Add the sauce and herbs to the spaghetti and toss to combine. Serve immediately, garnished with finely shredded lemon zest.

PREPARATION TIME: 10 MINUTES   COOKING TIME: 20 MINUTES

MEATBALLS WITH FUSILLI

750 g (1 lb 10 oz) minced (ground) pork
and veal or beef
80 g (2³/₄ oz/1 cup) fresh breadcrumbs
3 tablespoons freshly grated parmesan
cheese
1 onion, finely chopped
2 tablespoons chopped flat-leaf (Italian)
parsley
1 egg, beaten
1 garlic clove, crushed
zest and juice of ¹/₂ lemon
30 g (1 oz/¹/₄ cup) plain (all-purpose)
flour, seasoned
2 tablespoons olive oil
500 g (1 lb 2 oz) fusilli

SAUCE
425 g (15 oz) tinned tomato passata
(puréed tomatoes)
125 ml (4 fl oz/¹/₂ cup) beef stock
125 ml (4 fl oz/¹/₂ cup) red wine
2 tablespoons chopped basil
1 garlic clove, crushed

SERVES 4

Combine the meat, breadcrumbs, parmesan, onion, parsley, egg, garlic, lemon zest and juice in a large bowl and season to taste. Roll tablespoons of the mixture into balls and roll the balls in the seasoned flour.

Heat the oil in a large frying pan and fry the meatballs until golden. Remove from the pan and drain on paper towels. Remove the excess fat and meat juices from the pan.

To make the sauce, in the same pan, combine the tomato passata, stock, wine, basil, garlic, salt and pepper. Bring to the boil.

Reduce the heat and return the meatballs to the pan. Allow to simmer for 10–15 minutes.

While the meatballs and sauce are cooking, add the fusilli to a large saucepan of rapidly boiling salted water and cook until *al dente*. Drain and serve with meatballs and sauce over the top.

PREPARATION TIME: 35 MINUTES   COOKING TIME: 35 MINUTES

SEAFOOD RISOTTO

2 ripe tomatoes
500 g (1 lb 2 oz) black mussels
310 ml (10³/₄ fl oz/1¹/₄ cups) dry white wine
1.25 litres (44 fl oz/5 cups) fish stock
pinch saffron threads
2 tablespoons olive oil
30 g (1 oz) butter
500 g (1 lb 2 oz) raw prawns (shrimp), peeled and deveined
225 g (8 oz) squid tubes, sliced into thin rings
200 g (7 oz) scallops
3 garlic cloves, crushed
1 onion, finely chopped
370 g (13 oz/2 cups) risotto rice
2 tablespoons chopped flat-leaf (Italian) parsley

SERVES 4

Score a cross in the base of each tomato. Put in a heatproof bowl and cover with boiling water. Leave for 30 seconds, then transfer to cold water and peel the skin away from the cross. Chop the tomato flesh.

Scrub the mussels with a stiff brush and pull out the hairy beards. Discard any broken mussels, or open ones that don't close when tapped. Rinse well. Pour the wine into a large saucepan and bring to the boil. Add the mussels and cook, covered, over medium heat for 3–5 minutes, or until the mussels open. Discard any unopened mussels. Strain, reserving the liquid. Remove the mussels from their shells. Combine the mussel liquid, stock and saffron in a saucepan, cover and keep at a low simmer.

Heat the oil and butter in a saucepan over medium heat. Add the prawns and cook until pink. Remove. Add the squid and scallops and cook for about 1–2 minutes, until white. Remove. Add the garlic and onion and cook for 3 minutes, or until golden. Add the rice and stir. Add 125 ml (4 fl oz/¹/₂ cup) of the hot liquid, stirring until it is all absorbed. Continue adding liquid, 125 ml (4 fl oz/¹/₂ cup) at a time, stirring, for 25 minutes, or until the liquid is absorbed. Stir in the tomato, seafood and parsley and heat through. Season to taste.

PREPARATION TIME: 25 MINUTES   COOKING TIME: 45 MINUTES

CHEESE TORTELLINI WITH NUTTY HERB SAUCE

500 g (1 lb 2 oz) ricotta-filled fresh or dried tortellini or ravioli
60 g (2¹/₄ oz) butter
100 g (3¹/₂ oz) walnuts, finely chopped
100 g (3¹/₂ oz/²/₃ cup) pine nuts
2 tablespoons chopped flat-leaf (Italian) parsley
2 teaspoons thyme
60 g (2¹/₄ oz/¹/₄ cup) ricotta cheese
60 ml (2 fl oz/¹/₄ cup) pouring (whipping) cream

SERVES 4–6

Add the pasta to a large saucepan of rapidly boiling water and cook until *al dente*. Drain and return to the pan.

To make the sauce, heat the butter in a heavy-based frying pan over medium heat until foaming. Add the walnuts and pine nuts and stir for 5 minutes, or until golden brown. Add the parsley, thyme and season.

Beat the ricotta with the cream. Add the sauce to the pasta and toss well to combine. Top with a dollop of ricotta cream. Serve immediately.

PREPARATION TIME: 15 MINUTES   COOKING TIME: 15 MINUTES

Seafood risotto

CREAMY SEAFOOD RAVIOLI

PASTA
250 g (9 oz/2 cups) plain (all-purpose) flour
3 eggs
1 tablespoon olive oil
1 egg yolk, extra

FILLING
50 g (1³/4 oz) butter, softened
3 garlic cloves, finely chopped
2 tablespoons finely chopped flat-leaf (Italian) parsley
100 g (3¹/2 oz) scallops, cleaned and finely chopped
100 g (3¹/2 oz) raw prawn (shrimp) meat, finely chopped

SAUCE
70 g (2¹/2 oz) butter
3 tablespoons plain (all-purpose) flour
375 ml (13 fl oz/1¹/2 cups) milk
300 ml (10¹/2 fl oz) pouring (whipping) cream
125 ml (4 fl oz/¹/2 cup) dry white wine
50 g (1³/4 oz/¹/2 cup) freshly grated parmesan cheese
2 tablespoons chopped flat-leaf (Italian) parsley

SERVES 4

To make the pasta, sift the flour and a pinch of salt into a bowl and make a well in the centre. Whisk the eggs, oil and 1 tablespoon water in a bowl, then add gradually to the flour and mix to a firm dough. Gather into a ball.

Knead on a lightly floured surface for 5 minutes, or until smooth and elastic. Transfer to a lightly oiled bowl, cover with plastic wrap and set aside for 30 minutes.

To make the filling, mix together the softened butter, chopped garlic, parsley, scallops and prawn meat. Set aside.

Roll out a quarter of the pasta dough at a time until very thin (each portion of dough should be roughly 10 cm/4 inches wide when rolled). Place 1 teaspoonful of filling at 5 cm (2 inch) intervals down one side of each strip. Whisk the extra egg yolk with 60 ml (2 fl oz/¹/4 cup) water. Brush along one side of the dough and between the filling. Fold the dough over the filling to meet the other side. Repeat with the remaining filling and dough. Press the edges of the dough together firmly to seal.

Cut between the mounds with a knife or a fluted pastry cutter. Cook, in batches, in a large saucepan of rapidly boiling salted water for 6 minutes each batch. Drain well and return to the pan to keep warm.

To make the sauce, melt the butter in a saucepan, add the flour and cook over low heat for 2 minutes. Remove from the heat and gradually stir in the combined milk, cream and wine. Cook over low heat until the sauce begins to thicken, stirring constantly to prevent lumps forming. Bring to the boil and simmer gently for 5 minutes. Add the parmesan and parsley and stir until combined. Remove from the heat, add to the ravioli and toss well.

PREPARATION TIME: 1 HOUR +   COOKING TIME: 30 MINUTES

NOTE: The pasta dough is set aside for 30 minutes to let the gluten in the flour relax. If you don't do this, you run the risk of making tough pasta.

RED WINE RISOTTO

500 ml (17 fl oz/2 cups) chicken stock
100 g (3½ oz) butter
1 onion, finely chopped
1 large garlic clove, crushed
2 tablespoons chopped thyme
220 g (7¾ oz/1 cup) risotto rice
500 ml (17 fl oz/2 cups) dry red wine
50 g (1¾ oz/½ cup) freshly grated
parmesan cheese

SERVES 4 AS A STARTER

Pour the stock into a saucepan and bring to the boil. Reduce the heat, cover with a lid and keep at a low simmer.

Heat the butter in a large wide saucepan. Add the onion and garlic and cook until softened but not browned. Add the thyme and rice and stir until the rice is well coated. Season.

Add half the red wine and cook, stirring, until it has all been absorbed. Add 125 ml (4 fl oz/½ cup) of the hot stock and stir over medium heat until all the liquid is absorbed. Continue adding more stock, 125 ml (4 fl oz/½ cup) at a time until you have used half the stock. Add the remaining red wine to the risotto, stirring until it has been absorbed. Keep adding 125 ml (4 fl oz/½ cup) of the stock until all the liquid is absorbed and the rice is tender and creamy.

Remove the pan from the heat and stir in half the parmesan. Serve with the remaining cheese sprinkled over the top.

PREPARATION TIME: 20 MINUTES   COOKING TIME: 25 MINUTES

BAKED CHICKEN AND LEEK RISOTTO

60 g (2¼ oz) butter
1 leek, thinly sliced
2 boneless, skinless chicken breasts, cut
into 2 cm (¾ inch) cubes
440 g (15½ oz/2 cups) risotto rice
60 ml (2 fl oz/¼ cup) dry white wine
1.25 litres (44 fl oz/5 cups) chicken stock
35 g (1¼ oz/⅓ cup) freshly grated
parmesan cheese, plus extra, to serve
2 tablespoons thyme, plus extra,
to garnish

SERVES 4–6

Preheat the oven to 150°C (300°F/Gas 2) and place a 5 litre (160 fl oz/20-cup) ovenproof dish with a lid in the oven to warm. Heat the butter in a saucepan over medium heat. Add the leek and cook for 2 minutes, or until softened but not browned.

Add the chicken and cook, stirring, for 2–3 minutes, or until it colours. Add the rice and stir well. Cook for 1 minute.

Add the wine and stock and bring to the boil. Pour the mixture into the warm ovenproof dish and cover. Place in the oven and cook for 30 minutes, stirring halfway through. Remove from the oven and stir through the parmesan and thyme leaves. Season. Sprinkle with extra thyme and parmesan.

PREPARATION TIME: 10 MINUTES   COOKING TIME: 40 MINUTES

POTATO GNOCCHI WITH TOMATO AND BASIL SAUCE

TOMATO SAUCE
1 tablespoon oil
1 onion, chopped
1 celery stalk, chopped
2 carrots, chopped
850 g (1 lb 14 oz) tinned crushed tomatoes
1 teaspoon sugar
30 g (1 oz/½ cup) chopped basil

POTATO GNOCCHI
1 kg (2 lb 4 oz) all-purpose potatoes
30 g (1 oz) butter
250 g (9 oz/2 cups) plain (all-purpose) flour
2 eggs, beaten

freshly grated parmesan cheese, to serve

SERVES 4–6

To make the tomato sauce, heat the oil in a large frying pan, add the onion, celery and carrot and cook for 5 minutes, stirring regularly. Add the tomato and sugar and season to taste. Bring to the boil, reduce the heat to very low and simmer for 20 minutes. Cool slightly and process, in batches, in a food processor until smooth. Add the basil; set aside.

To make the potato gnocchi, peel the potatoes, chop roughly and steam or boil until very tender. Drain thoroughly and mash until smooth. Using a wooden spoon, stir in the butter and flour, then beat in the eggs. Cool.

Turn the gnocchi mixture onto a floured surface and divide into two. Roll each into a long sausage shape. Cut into short pieces and press each piece with the back of a fork.

Cook the gnocchi, in batches, in a large saucepan of boiling salted water for about 2 minutes, or until the gnocchi rise to the surface. Using a slotted spoon, drain the gnocchi, and transfer to serving bowls. Serve with the tomato sauce and freshly grated parmesan.

PREPARATION TIME: 1 HOUR   COOKING TIME: 50 MINUTES

LINGUINE PESTO

100 g (3½ oz) basil
2 garlic cloves, crushed
40 g (1½ oz/¼ cup) pine nuts, toasted
185 ml (6 fl oz/¾ cup) olive oil
50 g (1¾ oz/½ cup) freshly grated
parmesan cheese, plus extra, to serve
500 g (1 lb 2 oz) linguine

SERVES 4–6

Process the basil, garlic and pine nuts together in a food processor. With the motor running, add the oil in a steady stream until mixed to a smooth paste. Transfer to a bowl, stir in the parmesan and season to taste.

Cook the pasta in a large saucepan of rapidly boiling salted water until *al dente*. Drain and return to the pan. Toss enough of the pesto through the pasta to coat it well. Serve sprinkled with parmesan.

PREPARATION TIME: 15 MINUTES   COOKING TIME: 15 MINUTES

NOTE: Refrigerate any leftover pesto in an airtight jar for up to a week. Cover the surface with a layer of oil. Freeze for up to 1 month.

FETTUCINE PRIMAVERA

500 g (1 lb 2 oz) fettucine
150 g (5½ oz) fresh asparagus spears
155 g (5½ oz/1 cup) frozen or fresh
broad (fava) beans
30 g (1 oz) butter
1 celery stalk, sliced
155 g (5½ oz/1 cup) peas
310 ml (10 fl oz/1¼ cups) pouring
(whipping) cream
50 g (1¾ oz/½ cup) freshly grated
parmesan cheese

SERVES 6

Cook the pasta in a large saucepan of rapidly boiling salted water until *al dente*. Drain and return to the pan.

Cut the asparagus into small pieces. Bring a saucepan of water to the boil, add the asparagus and cook for 2 minutes. Using a slotted spoon, remove the asparagus from the pan and plunge the pieces into a bowl of ice cold water.

Add the frozen broad beans to the saucepan of boiling water. Remove immediately and cool in cold water. Drain, then peel and discard any rough outside skin. If fresh broad beans are used, cook them for 2–5 minutes or until tender. If the beans are young, the skin can be left on, but old beans should be peeled.

Heat the butter in a heavy-based frying pan. Add the celery and stir for 2 minutes. Add the peas and the cream and cook gently for 3 minutes. Add the asparagus, broad beans, parmesan, and season to taste. Bring the sauce to the boil and cook for 1 minute. Add the sauce to the cooked fettucine and toss well to combine.

PREPARATION TIME: 35 MINUTES   COOKING TIME: 25 MINUTES

PASTICCIO

250 g (9 oz/2 cups) plain (all-purpose) flour
125 g (4¹⁄₂ oz) cold butter, chopped
55 g (2 oz/¹⁄₄ cup) caster (superfine) sugar
1 egg yolk
150 g (5¹⁄₂ oz) bucatini or penne

FILLING
2 tablespoons olive oil
1 onion, chopped
2 garlic cloves, finely chopped
500 g (1 lb 2 oz) minced (ground) beef
150 g (5¹⁄₂ oz) chicken livers
2 tomatoes, chopped
125 ml (4 fl oz/¹⁄₂ cup) red wine
125 ml (4 fl oz/¹⁄₂ cup) rich beef stock
1 tablespoon chopped oregano
¹⁄₄ teaspoon freshly grated nutmeg
50 g (1³⁄₄ oz/¹⁄₂ cup) freshly grated parmesan cheese

BÉCHAMEL SAUCE
60 g (2¹⁄₄ oz) butter
2 tablespoons plain (all-purpose) flour
375 ml (12 fl oz/1¹⁄₂ cups) cold milk

SERVES 6

Put the flour, butter, sugar and egg yolk in a food processor with 1 tablespoon water. Process lightly until the mixture forms a ball, adding more water if necessary. Lightly knead the dough on a floured surface until smooth. Wrap in plastic wrap and refrigerate.

To make the filling, heat the oil in a heavy-based saucepan and cook the onion and garlic until softened and lightly golden. Increase the heat, add the beef and cook until browned, breaking up any lumps with a fork. Add the livers, tomato, red wine, stock, oregano and nutmeg, then season well. Cook the sauce over high heat until it boils, then reduce to a simmer and cook, covered, for 40 minutes, then cool. Stir in the parmesan.

To make the béchamel sauce, heat the butter in a saucepan over low heat. Add the flour and stir for 1 minute, or until the mixture is golden and smooth. Remove from the heat and gradually stir in the milk. Return to the heat and stir constantly until the sauce boils and begins to thicken. Simmer for another minute. Season to taste.

Cook the bucatini in a saucepan of rapidly boiling salted water until *al dente*. Drain and cool.

Preheat the oven to 160°C (315°F/Gas 2–3). Lightly grease a 23 cm (9 inch) deep pie dish. Divide the dough into two and roll out one piece to fit the base of the prepared dish, overlapping the sides. Spoon about half of the meat mixture into the dish, top with the bucatini and slowly spoon the béchamel sauce over the top, allowing it to seep down and coat the bucatini. Top with the remaining meat. Roll out the remaining dough and cover the pie. Trim the edges and pinch lightly to seal. Bake for 50–55 minutes, or until dark golden brown and crisp. Set aside for 15 minutes before cutting.

PREPARATION TIME: 1 HOUR   COOKING TIME: 1 HOUR 50 MINUTES

RISI E BISI

1.5 litres (52 fl oz/6 cups) chicken or vegetable stock
2 teaspoons olive oil
40 g (1½ oz) butter
1 small onion, finely chopped
80 g (2¾ oz) pancetta, cubed
2 tablespoons chopped flat-leaf (Italian) parsley
375 g (13 oz) young peas
220 g (7¾ oz/1 cup) risotto rice
50 g (1¾ oz/½ cup) freshly grated parmesan cheese

SERVES 4

Pour the stock into a saucepan and bring to the boil. Reduce the heat, cover with a lid and keep at a low simmer.

Heat the oil and half the butter in a large wide heavy-based saucepan and cook the onion and pancetta over low heat for 5 minutes until softened. Stir in the parsley and peas and add two ladlefuls of the stock. Simmer for 6–8 minutes.

Add the rice and the remaining stock. Simmer until the rice is *al dente* and most of the stock has been absorbed. Stir in the remaining butter and the parmesan, season and serve.

PREPARATION TIME: 15 MINUTES   COOKING TIME: 25 MINUTES

GARLIC BUCATINI

500 g (1 lb 2 oz) bucatini or penne
80 ml (2½ fl oz/⅓ cup) olive oil
8 garlic cloves, crushed
2 tablespoons chopped flat-leaf (Italian) parsley
freshly grated parmesan cheese, to serve

SERVES 4

Cook the bucatini in a large saucepan of rapidly boiling water until *al dente*. Drain and return to the pan.

Heat the olive oil over low heat in a frying pan and add the garlic. Cook for 1 minute before removing from the heat. Add the garlic oil and the parsley to the pasta and toss to distribute thoroughly. Serve with parmesan cheese.

PREPARATION TIME: 10 MINUTES   COOKING TIME: 20 MINUTES

SPAGHETTI MARINARA

12 mussels

TOMATO SAUCE
2 tablespoons olive oil
1 onion, finely diced
1 carrot, sliced
1 red chilli, seeded and chopped
2 garlic cloves, crushed
425 g (15 oz) tinned crushed tomatoes
125 ml (4 fl oz/½ cup) dry white wine
1 teaspoon sugar
pinch cayenne pepper

60 ml (2 fl oz/¼ cup) white wine
60 ml (2 fl oz/¼ cup) fish stock
1 garlic clove, crushed
375 g (13 oz) spaghetti
30 g (1 oz) butter
125 g (4½ oz) small squid tubes, sliced
125 g (4½ oz) boneless white fish fillets, cubed
200 g (7 oz) raw prawns (shrimp), peeled and deveined
1 large handful flat-leaf (Italian) parsley, chopped
200 g (7 oz) tinned clams, drained

SERVES 6

Scrub the mussels with a stiff brush and pull out the hairy beards. Discard any broken mussels, or open ones that don't close when tapped on the bench. Rinse well.

To make the tomato sauce, heat the oil in a saucepan, add the onion and carrot and stir over medium heat for about 10 minutes, or until the vegetables are lightly browned. Add the chilli, garlic, tomato, white wine, sugar and cayenne pepper. Simmer for 30 minutes, stirring occasionally.

Meanwhile, heat the wine with the stock and garlic in a large saucepan and add the unopened mussels. Cover the pan and shake it over high heat for 3–5 minutes. After 3 minutes, start removing any opened mussels and set them aside. After 5 minutes discard any unopened mussels and reserve the wine mixture.

Cook the pasta in a large saucepan of rapidly boiling salted water until *al dente*. Drain and keep warm. Meanwhile, melt the butter in a frying pan, add the squid rings, fish and prawns and stir-fry for 2 minutes. Set aside. Add the reserved wine mixture, mussels, squid, fish, prawns, parsley and clams to the tomato sauce and reheat gently. Gently combine the sauce with the pasta and serve at once.

PREPARATION TIME: 40 MINUTES   COOKING TIME: 50 MINUTES

SPAGHETTINI WITH GARLIC AND CHILLI

500 g (1 lb 2 oz) spaghettini
125 ml (4 fl oz/$\frac{1}{2}$ cup) extra virgin olive oil
2–3 garlic cloves, finely chopped
1–2 red chillies, seeded and finely chopped
3 tablespoons chopped flat-leaf (Italian) parsley
freshly grated parmesan cheese, to serve

SERVES 4–6

Cook the spaghettini in a large saucepan of rapidly boiling salted water until *al dente*. Drain and return to the pan.

Meanwhile, heat the extra virgin olive oil in a large frying pan. Add the garlic and chilli, and cook over very low heat for 2–3 minutes, or until the garlic is golden. Take care not to burn the garlic or chilli as this will make the sauce bitter.

Toss the parsley and the warmed oil, garlic and chilli mixture through the pasta. Season. Serve with the parmesan.

PREPARATION TIME: 10 MINUTES   COOKING TIME: 20 MINUTES

SPAGHETTI BOLOGNESE

2 tablespoons olive oil
2 garlic cloves, crushed
1 large onion, chopped
1 carrot, chopped
1 celery stalk, chopped
500 g (1 lb 2 oz) minced (ground) beef
500 ml (17 fl oz/2 cups) beef stock
375 ml (13 fl oz/1$\frac{1}{2}$ cups) red wine
850 g (1 lb 14 oz) tinned crushed tomatoes
1 teaspoon sugar
3 tablespoons chopped flat-leaf (Italian) parsley
500 g (1 lb 2 oz) spaghetti
freshly grated parmesan cheese, to serve

SERVES 4–6

Heat the olive oil in a large deep frying pan. Add the garlic, onion, carrot and celery and stir for 5 minutes over low heat until the vegetables are golden.

Increase the heat, add the beef and brown well, stirring and breaking up any lumps with a fork as it cooks. Add the stock, wine, tomato, sugar and parsley.

Bring the mixture to the boil, reduce the heat and simmer for 1$\frac{1}{2}$ hours, stirring occasionally. Season to taste.

While the sauce is cooking and shortly before serving, cook the pasta in a large saucepan of rapidly boiling salted water until *al dente*. Drain and then divide among serving bowls. Serve the sauce over the top of the pasta and sprinkle with the freshly grated parmesan cheese.

PREPARATION TIME: 20 MINUTES   COOKING TIME: 1 HOUR 40 MINUTES

TIMBALLO OF LEEKS, ZUCCHINI AND BASIL

pinch saffron threads

125 ml (4 fl oz/^{1}/$_2$ cup) dry white wine

750 ml (26 fl oz/3 cups) chicken stock

50 g (1^3/$_4$ oz) butter

1 onion, finely chopped

2 garlic cloves, crushed

360 g (12^3/$_4$ oz/1^2/$_3$ cups) risotto rice

leaves from 2 thyme sprigs

50 g (1^3/$_4$ oz/^{1}/$_2$ cup) freshly grated parmesan cheese

2 tablespoons olive oil

2 leeks, thinly sliced

400 g (14 oz) thin zucchini (courgettes), thinly sliced on the diagonal

^{1}/$_4$ teaspoon freshly grated nutmeg

10 basil leaves, shredded

70 g (2^1/$_2$ oz) thinly sliced prosciutto, cut into strips

90 g (3^1/$_4$ oz/^{1}/$_3$ cup) sour cream

SERVES 4–6

Soak the saffron in the wine. Pour the stock and 125 ml (4 fl oz/^{1}/$_2$ cup) water into a saucepan and bring to the boil. Reduce the heat, cover with a lid and keep at a low simmer.

Melt half the butter in a large saucepan wider than it is high. Add the onion and garlic and cook over low heat for about 5 minutes, or until softened but not browned. Add the rice and stir until well coated. Stir in the thyme and season well. Stir in the saffron-infused wine, then increase the heat and cook, stirring constantly, until it is absorbed. Stir 125 ml (4 fl oz/^{1}/$_2$ cup) of the stock into the rice, then reduce the heat and cook until it is absorbed. Continue adding more liquid, 125 ml (4 fl oz/^{1}/$_2$ cup) at a time until all the liquid is absorbed and the rice is tender and creamy. This will take around 25–30 minutes. Remove from the heat and stir in the remaining butter and the parmesan.

Heat the oil in a frying pan and cook the leek without browning over low heat for 5 minutes. Add the zucchini slices and cook for about 5 minutes, or until softened. Add the nutmeg and season well. Stir in the basil, prosciutto and sour cream. Cook, stirring, for 2–3 minutes, or until the sauce thickens.

Preheat the oven to 180°C (350°F/Gas 4) and grease a 1.5 litre (52 fl oz/ 6-cup) pudding basin (mould) or rounded ovenproof bowl. Cut out a piece of greaseproof paper the size of the basin's base and line the base. Cover with half the rice mixture, pressing it down firmly. Spoon in two-thirds of the zucchini mixture, keeping the remaining one-third warm in the pan. Press in the last of the rice mixture. Cover with foil and transfer to the oven.

Bake for 20 minutes. Remove from the oven and rest for 5 minutes. Carefully unmould onto a serving plate. Serve the reserved zucchini on the side and serve.

PREPARATION TIME: 15 MINUTES   COOKING TIME: 1 HOUR 10 MINUTES

NOTE: The prosciutto can be eliminated and the stock changed to vegetable if you'd prefer a vegetarian version.

CREAMY BOSCAIOLA

500 g (1 lb 2 oz) pasta
1 tablespoon olive oil
6 bacon slices, chopped
200 g (7 oz) button mushrooms, sliced
625 ml (21/2 fl oz/21/2 cups) pouring
(whipping) cream
2 spring onions (scallions), sliced
1 tablespoon chopped flat-leaf
(Italian) parsley

SERVES 4

Cook the pasta in a large saucepan of rapidly boiling salted water until *al dente*. Drain, return to the pan and keep warm.

While the pasta is cooking, heat the oil in a large frying pan, add the bacon and mushroom and cook, stirring, for 5 minutes, or until golden brown.

Stir in a little of the cream and scrape the wooden spoon on the bottom of the pan to dislodge any bacon that has stuck.

Add the remaining cream, bring to the boil and cook over high heat for 15 minutes, or until the sauce is thick enough to coat the back of a spoon. Stir the spring onion through the mixture. Pour the sauce over the pasta and toss to combine. Serve sprinkled with the parsley.

PREPARATION TIME: 15 MINUTES   COOKING TIME: 25 MINUTES

NOTE: This sauce is normally served with spaghetti, but you can use any pasta. We have shown it with parpadelle.

GORGONZOLA AND TOASTED WALNUTS ON LINGUINE

75 g (21/2 oz/3/4 cup) walnut halves
500 g (1 lb 2 oz) linguine
70 g (21/2 oz) butter
150 g (51/2 oz) gorgonzola cheese,
crumbled
2 tablespoons pouring (whipping) cream
155 g (51/2 oz/1 cup) fresh peas

SERVES 4

Preheat the oven to 180°C (350°F/Gas 4). Lay the walnuts on a baking tray in a single layer and bake for about 5 minutes, until lightly toasted. Set the walnuts aside to cool.

Cook the linguine in a large saucepan of rapidly boiling water until *al dente*. Drain and return to the pan.

While the pasta is cooking, melt the butter in a small saucepan over low heat and add the gorgonzola, cream and peas. Stir gently for 5 minutes, or until the sauce has thickened. Season to taste. Add the sauce and the walnuts to the pasta and toss until well combined. Serve immediately, sprinkled with freshly ground black pepper.

PREPARATION TIME: 15 MINUTES   COOKING TIME: 20 MINUTES

FENNEL RISOTTO BALLS WITH CHEESY FILLING

1.5 litres (52 fl oz/6 cups) vegetable stock
1 tablespoon oil
30 g (1 oz) butter
2 garlic cloves, crushed
1 onion, finely chopped
2 fennel bulbs, thinly sliced
1 tablespoon balsamic vinegar
125 ml (4 fl oz/$\frac{1}{2}$ cup) dry white wine
660 g (1 lb 7 oz/3 cups) risotto rice
50 g (1$\frac{3}{4}$ oz/$\frac{1}{2}$ cup) freshly grated parmesan cheese
25 g (1 oz/$\frac{1}{2}$ cup) snipped chives
1 egg, lightly beaten
150 g (5$\frac{1}{2}$ oz) sun-dried (sun-blushed) tomatoes, chopped
100 g (3$\frac{1}{2}$ oz) mozzarella cheese, cubed
80 g (2$\frac{3}{4}$ oz/$\frac{1}{2}$ cup) frozen peas, thawed
60 g (2$\frac{1}{4}$ oz/$\frac{1}{2}$ cup) plain (all-purpose) flour, seasoned
3 eggs, extra
200 g (7 oz/2 cups) dry breadcrumbs
oil, for deep-frying

SERVES 4–6

Pour the stock into a saucepan and bring to the boil. Reduce the heat, cover with a lid and keep at a low simmer.

Heat the oil and butter in a large saucepan and cook the garlic and onion over medium heat for 3 minutes, or until softened but not browned. Add the fennel and cook for 10 minutes, or until it starts to caramelize. Add the vinegar and wine, increase the heat and boil until the liquid evaporates. Stir in the rice until well coated.

Add 125 ml (4 fl oz/$\frac{1}{2}$ cup) hot stock, stirring constantly over medium heat until the liquid is absorbed. Continue adding more stock, 125 ml (4 fl oz/$\frac{1}{2}$ cup) at a time, stirring, for 20–25 minutes, or until all the stock is absorbed and the rice is tender and creamy.

Remove from the heat and stir in the parmesan, chives, egg and tomato. Transfer to a bowl, cover and cool. Put the mozzarella and peas in a bowl and mash together. Season.

Put the flour in one bowl, the extra eggs in another and the breadcrumbs in a third. Lightly beat the eggs. With wet hands, shape the risotto into 14 even balls. Flatten each ball out, slightly indenting the centre. Put a heaped teaspoon of the pea mash into the indentation, then shape the rice around the filling to form a ball. Roll each ball in seasoned flour, then dip in the extra egg and roll in breadcrumbs. Place on a foil-covered tray and refrigerate for 30 minutes.

Fill a deep-fat fryer or large saucepan one-third full of oil and heat to 180°C (350°F), or until a cube of bread dropped into the oil browns in 15 seconds. Cook the risotto balls in batches for 5 minutes, or until golden and crisp and the cheese has melted inside. Drain on crumpled paper towels and season with salt. If the cheese has not melted by the end of the cooking time, cook the balls on a tray in a 180°C/350°F/Gas 4 oven for 5 minutes. Serve with a salad.

PREPARATION TIME: 30 MINUTES +   COOKING TIME: 50 MINUTES

ORECCHIETTE WITH TUNA, LEMON AND CAPER SAUCE

500 g (1 lb 2 oz) orecchiette
30 g (1 oz) butter
1 garlic clove, crushed
1 onion, finely chopped
425 g (15 oz) tinned tuna in brine, drained
2 tablespoons lemon juice
250 ml (9 fl oz/1 cup) pouring (whipping) cream
2 tablespoons chopped flat-leaf (Italian) parsley
1 tablespoon capers, drained
¼ teaspoon cayenne pepper (optional)
caperberries, to garnish (optional)

SERVES 4

Cook the orecchiette in a large saucepan of rapidly boiling salted water until *al dente*. Drain and return to the pan.

Heat the butter in a saucepan and cook the garlic and onion for 1–2 minutes. Add the tuna, lemon juice, cream, half the parsley and the capers. Season with black pepper and cayenne, if using. Simmer over low heat for 5 minutes.

Add the tuna sauce to the pasta and toss until thoroughly combined. Serve the pasta sprinkled with the remaining parsley. Garnish with caperberries, if desired.

PREPARATION TIME: 10 MINUTES   COOKING TIME: 20 MINUTES

CREAMY PRAWNS WITH FETTUCINE

500 g (1 lb 2 oz) fettucine
500 g (1 lb 2 oz) raw prawns (shrimp)
30 g (1 oz) butter
1 tablespoon olive oil
6 spring onions (scallions), chopped
1 garlic clove, crushed
250 ml (9 fl oz/1 cup) pouring (whipping) cream
2 tablespoons chopped flat-leaf (Italian) parsley, to serve

SERVES 4

Cook the fettucine in a large saucepan of rapidly boiling water until *al dente*. Drain and return to the pan.

Peel the prawns and gently pull out the dark vein from each prawn back, starting from the head end. Heat the butter and oil in a frying pan, add the spring onion and garlic and stir over low heat for 1 minute. Add the prawns and cook for 2–3 minutes, or until the flesh changes colour. Remove the prawns from the pan and set aside. Add the cream to the pan and bring to the boil. Reduce the heat and simmer until the sauce begins to thicken. Return the prawns to the pan, season to taste, and simmer for 1 minute.

Add the prawns and sauce to the warm fettucine and toss gently. Serve sprinkled with chopped parsley.

PREPARATION TIME: 30 MINUTES   COOKING TIME: 20 MINUTES

Orecchiette with tuna, lemon and caper sauce

SPINACH RISOTTO CAKE

250 g (9 oz) baby English spinach leaves
750 ml (26 fl oz/3 cups) chicken stock
100 g (3^1/2 oz) butter
1 onion, finely chopped
1 garlic clove, finely chopped
220 g (7^3/4 oz/1 cup) risotto rice
150 ml (5 fl oz) dry white vermouth or white wine
^{1}/4 teaspoon freshly grated nutmeg
25 g (1 oz/^{1}/4 cup) freshly grated parmesan cheese, plus extra, to serve

SERVES 6

Cook the spinach in a small amount of salted water until just wilted. Refresh in cold water and squeeze dry. Finely chop and set aside.

Pour the stock into a saucepan and bring to the boil. Reduce the heat, cover with a lid and keep at a low simmer.

Melt 70 g (2^1/2 oz) of the butter in a deep heavy-based frying pan and gently cook the onion and garlic until softened but not browned. Stir in the rice until well coated. Season.

Add the vermouth to the rice and cook, stirring, until all the liquid has been absorbed. Add 125 ml (4 fl oz/^{1}/2 cup) of the hot stock and stir constantly over medium heat until all the liquid is absorbed. Continue adding more stock, 125 ml (4 fl oz/^{1}/2 cup) at a time until a quarter of the stock is left, then mix in the chopped spinach. Continue to add the last of the stock.

Remove the pan from the heat and stir in the nutmeg, parmesan cheese and the remaining butter.

Smear a little butter into a mould such as a 1.25 litre (44 fl oz/5-cup) cake tin. Spoon the risotto into the mould, pressing it down firmly. Leave to rest for 5 minutes, then unmould and put on a warm serving plate with some parmesan sprinkled over the top.

PREPARATION TIME: 30 MINUTES   COOKING TIME: 35 MINUTES

NOTE: Serve with a rich meat dish such as osso bucco.

PENNE ARRABBIATA

75 g (2¹/₂ oz) bacon fat
2–3 red chillies
2 tablespoons olive oil
1 large onion, finely chopped
1 garlic clove, finely chopped
500 g (1 lb 2 oz) very ripe tomatoes, finely chopped
500 g (1 lb 2 oz) penne
2 tablespoons chopped flat-leaf (Italian) parsley
freshly grated parmesan or pecorino cheese, to serve (optional)

SERVES 4

Use a large knife to finely chop the bacon fat. Chop the chillies, taking care to avoid skin irritation — wearing rubber gloves will help. Heat the oil in a heavy-based frying pan and add the bacon fat, chilli, onion and garlic. Cook for 8 minutes over medium heat, stirring occasionally.

Add the chopped tomato along with 125 ml (4 fl oz/¹/₂ cup) water and season to taste. Cover and simmer for about 40 minutes, or until the sauce is thick and rich.

When the sauce is almost cooked, cook the pasta in a large saucepan of rapidly boiling salted water until *al dente*. Drain and return to the pan.

Add the parsley to the sauce. Taste and season again, if necessary. Pour the sauce over the pasta in the pan and toss gently. Serve with the freshly grated parmesan or pecorino cheese sprinkled over the top, if desired.

PREPARATION TIME: 30 MINUTES   COOKING TIME: 50 MINUTES

SPAGHETTI VONGOLE

1 kg (2 lb 4 oz) small clams in shell or 750 g (1 lb 10 oz) tinned clams in brine
1 tablespoon lemon juice
80 ml (2¹/₂ fl oz/¹/₃ cup) olive oil
3 garlic cloves, crushed
850 g (1 lb 14 oz) tinned crushed tomatoes
250 g (9 oz) spaghetti
4 tablespoons chopped flat-leaf (Italian) parsley

SERVES 4

If using fresh clams, clean thoroughly. Place in a large saucepan with the lemon juice. Cover the pan and shake over medium heat for 7–8 minutes until the shells open, discarding any that don't open. Remove the clam flesh from the shell of the opened clams and set aside; discard the empty shells. If using canned clams, drain, rinse well and set aside.

Heat the oil in a large saucepan. Add the garlic and cook over low heat for 5 minutes. Add the tomato and stir to combine. Bring to the boil and simmer, covered, for 20 minutes. Add freshly ground black pepper, to taste, and the clams, and stir until heated through.

While the sauce is cooking, cook the spaghetti in a large saucepan of rapidly boiling salted water until *al dente*. Drain and return to the pan. Gently stir in the sauce and the chopped parsley until combined.

PREPARATION TIME: 25 MINUTES   COOKING TIME: 35 MINUTES

BAKED CHEESE AND SPINACH CANNELLONI

TOMATO SAUCE
2 tablespoons olive oil
1 large onion, finely chopped
2 garlic cloves, finely chopped
1.25 kg (2 lb 12 oz) tinned tomatoes,
roughly chopped
2 rosemary sprigs
2 bay leaves
2 tablespoons tomato paste
(concentrated purée)

500 g (1 lb 2 oz) English spinach
150 g (5½ oz) feta cheese, crumbled
150 g (5½ oz) ricotta cheese
50 g (1¾ oz/½ cup) freshly grated
parmesan cheese
2 tablespoons finely chopped mint
2 eggs, lightly beaten
2 tablespoons pine nuts, toasted
16 instant cannelloni tubes
200 g (7 oz) mozzarella cheese, finely
grated

SERVES 4

To make the tomato sauce, heat the olive oil in a large pan. Add the onion and garlic and cook over medium heat until the onion is soft. Add the tomato, herbs and tomato paste and mix thoroughly. Bring to the boil, reduce the heat and simmer for 25–30 minutes until the sauce is thick. Season to taste. Remove the bay leaves and rosemary sprigs and discard.

Preheat the oven to 200°C (400°F/Gas 6). Wash and remove the stems from the spinach. Steam until just wilted. Drain thoroughly and chop roughly. Combine the spinach with the ricotta and parmesan cheeses, mint, beaten eggs, pine nuts and season. Mix thoroughly. Using a small spoon or knife, carefully fill the cannelloni tubes.

Spoon some tomato sauce over the base of a large, shallow baking dish. Arrange cannelloni shells on top. Cover with remaining tomato sauce and mozzarella. Bake for 30–40 minutes, or until the top is golden and the pasta is tender.

PREPARATION TIME: 40 MINUTES   COOKING TIME: 1 HOUR 20 MINUTES

TAGLIATELLE WITH VEAL, WINE AND CREAM

500 g (1 lb 2 oz) veal scaloppine or escalopes, cut into thin strips
plain (all-purpose) flour, seasoned
60 g (2¼ oz) butter
1 onion, sliced
125 ml (4 fl oz/½ cup) dry white wine
60 ml (2 fl oz/¼ cup) beef stock or chicken stock
170 ml (5½ fl oz/⅔ cup) pouring (whipping) cream
600 g (1 lb 5 oz) fresh plain or spinach tagliatelle (or a mixture of both)
1 tablespoon freshly grated parmesan cheese, plus extra, to serve (optional)
flat-leaf (Italian) parsley, to garnish

SERVES 4

Coat the veal strips with the seasoned flour. Melt the butter in a frying pan. Add the veal strips and fry quickly until browned. Remove with a slotted spoon and set aside.

Add the onion slices to the pan and stir until soft and golden. Pour in the wine and cook rapidly to reduce the liquid. Add the stock and cream and season to taste. Reduce the sauce again, and add the veal towards the end.

Meanwhile, cook the tagliatelle in a large saucepan of rapidly boiling salted water until *al dente*. Drain and transfer to a warm serving dish.

Stir the parmesan through the sauce. Pour the sauce over the pasta. Serve with extra parmesan, if desired, and garnish with flat-leaf parsley.

PREPARATION TIME: 15 MINUTES   COOKING TIME: 20 MINUTES

FARFALLE WITH TUNA, MUSHROOMS AND CREAM

60 g (2¼ oz) butter
1 tablespoon olive oil
1 onion, chopped
1 garlic clove, crushed
125 g (4½ oz) button mushrooms, sliced
250 ml (9 fl oz/1 cup) pouring (whipping) cream
450 g (1 lb) tinned tuna in brine, drained and flaked
1 tablespoon lemon juice
1 tablespoon chopped flat-leaf (Italian) parsley
500 g (1 lb 2 oz) farfalle

SERVES 4

Heat the butter and olive oil in a large frying pan. Add the onion and garlic and stir over low heat for 3–5 minutes, until the onion is soft. Add the mushrooms and cook for 2 minutes. Pour in the cream, bring to the boil, then reduce the heat and simmer until the sauce begins to thicken. Add the tuna, lemon juice and parsley and stir until heated through. Season to taste.

While the sauce is cooking, add the farfalle to a large saucepan of rapidly boiling water and cook until *al dente*. Drain thoroughly, then return to the pan. Add the sauce to the farfalle and toss to combine.

PREPARATION TIME: 10 MINUTES   COOKING TIME: 15 MINUTES

NOTE: You can use tinned salmon, drained and flaked, instead of tuna.

Tagliatelle with veal, wine and cream

SEAFOOD LASAGNE

250 g (9 oz) instant lasagne sheets
125 g (4½ oz) scallops
500 g (1 lb 2 oz) raw prawns (shrimp)
500 g (1 lb 2 oz) skinless firm white fish
fillets (such as hake, snapper, flake,
gemfish or ling)
125 g (4½ oz) butter
1 leek, thinly sliced
85 g (3 oz/⅔ cup) plain (all-purpose) flour
500 ml (17 fl oz/2 cups) milk
500 ml (17 fl oz/2 cups) dry white wine
125 g (4½ oz) cheddar cheese, grated
125 ml (4 fl oz/½ cup) pouring (whipping)
cream
60 g (2¼ oz) parmesan cheese, grated
2 tablespoons chopped flat-leaf (Italian)
parsley

SERVES 4–6

Preheat the oven to 180°C (350°F/Gas 4). Line a greased shallow ovenproof dish (about 30 cm/12 inches square) with lasagne sheets, gently breaking them to fill any gaps. Set aside.

Slice or pull off any vein, membrane or hard white muscle from the scallops, leaving any roe attached.

Peel the prawns and gently pull out the dark vein from each prawn back, starting from the head end. Chop the seafood into even-sized pieces.

Melt the butter in a large saucepan over low heat, add the leek and cook, stirring, over medium heat for 1 minute, or until starting to soften. Stir in the flour and cook for 1 minute, or until pale and foaming. Remove from the heat and gradually stir in the combined milk and wine. Return to the heat and stir constantly over medium heat until the sauce boils and thickens. Reduce the heat and simmer for 2 minutes. Add the seafood and simmer for 1 minute. Remove from the heat, stir in the cheese, then season.

Spoon half the seafood mixture over the lasagne sheets in the dish, then top with another layer of lasagne sheets. Spoon the remaining seafood mixture over the lasagne sheets, then cover with another layer of lasagne sheets.

Pour the cream over the top, then sprinkle with the combined parmesan and parsley. Bake, uncovered, for 30 minutes, or until bubbling and golden brown.

PREPARATION TIME: 15 MINUTES   COOKING TIME: 45 MINUTES

SALMON AND PASTA FRITTATA

150 g (5½ oz) spaghettini
300 g (10½ oz) frozen broad (fava) beans
30 g (1 oz) butter
1 leek, thinly sliced
415 g (14¾ oz) tinned red salmon, drained, boned and flaked
6 eggs, lightly beaten
125 ml (4 fl oz/½ cup) pouring (whipping) cream
185 ml (6 fl oz/¾ cup) milk

SERVES 6

Add the pasta to a saucepan of boiling water and boil until *al dente*, then drain. Put the broad beans in a bowl, cover with boiling water and leave for 10 minutes. Drain, then remove and discard the outer skins.

Melt the butter in a saucepan, add the leek and cook, stirring over medium heat until soft. Mix the pasta, broad beans, leek, salmon, egg, cream and milk in a bowl. Season to taste.

Pour the mixture into a lightly greased 25 cm (10 inch) frying pan. Cover with a lid and cook over low heat for 25 minutes, or until nearly set.

Meanwhile, heat the grill (broiler). Place the frying pan under the grill and grill until the top has set. Set aside for 5 minutes. Cut into wedges directly from the pan. Serve with a leafy green salad.

PREPARATION TIME: 25 MINUTES   COOKING TIME: 40 MINUTES

SALMON AND LEMON CANNELLONI

FILLING
415 g (14¾ oz) tinned pink salmon
250 g (9 oz) ricotta cheese
1 tablespoon lemon juice
1 egg yolk, lightly beaten
2 tablespoons finely chopped onion

SAUCE
125 g (4½ oz) butter
85 g (3 oz/⅔ cup) plain (all-purpose) flour
685 ml (23½ fl oz/2¾ cups) milk
1 teaspoon finely grated lemon zest
¼ teaspoon freshly grated nutmeg

16 cannelloni tubes

SERVES 4–6

Drain the salmon, reserving the liquid for the sauce. Remove and discard the skin and bones. Flake the salmon flesh and mix with the ricotta, lemon juice, egg yolk and onion in a bowl. Season to taste.

To make the sauce, melt the butter in a saucepan over low heat. Stir in the flour and cook for 1 minute, or until pale and foaming. Remove from the heat and gradually stir in the milk. Return to the heat and stir constantly until the sauce boils and thickens. Reduce the heat and simmer for 2 minutes. Add the reserved salmon liquid, lemon zest and nutmeg, and season to taste. Set aside to cool.

Preheat the oven to 180°C (350°F/Gas 4). Fill the cannelloni tubes with filling, using a small spoon or piping bag. Spread one-third of the sauce over the bottom of a shallow ovenproof dish, then sit the cannelloni tubes in the dish side-by-side. Pour the remaining sauce over the top, covering all the exposed pasta. Bake for about 30 minutes, until bubbly.

PREPARATION TIME: 25 MINUTES   COOKING TIME: 40 MINUTES

Salmon and pasta frittata

LEMON, HERB AND FISH RISOTTO

60 g (2¼ oz) butter
400 g (14 oz) skinless firm white fish fillets
(such as coley, cod, blue-eye, ling),
cut into 3 cm (1¼ inch) cubes
1.25 litres (44 fl oz/5 cups) fish stock
1 onion, finely chopped
1 garlic clove, crushed
1 teaspoon ground turmeric
330 g (11¾ oz/1½ cups) risotto rice
2 tablespoons lemon juice
1 tablespoon chopped flat-leaf (Italian)
parsley
1 tablespoon snipped chives
1 tablespoon chopped dill

SERVES 4

Melt half the butter in a frying pan. Add the fish in batches and fry over medium–high heat for 3 minutes, or until the fish is just cooked through. Remove from the pan and set aside.

Pour the fish stock into another saucepan, bring to the boil, cover and keep at simmering point.

To the first pan, add the remaining butter, onion and garlic and cook over medium heat for 3 minutes, or until the onion is tender. Add the turmeric and stir for 1 minute. Add the rice and stir to coat, then add 125 ml (4 fl oz/½ cup) of the fish stock and cook, stirring constantly, over low heat until all the stock has been absorbed. Continue adding 125 ml (4 fl oz/½ cup) of stock at a time until all the stock has been added and the rice is translucent, tender and creamy.

Stir in the lemon juice, parsley, chives and dill. Add the fish and stir gently. Serve garnished with slices of lemon or lime and herb sprigs.

PREPARATION TIME: 20 MINUTES   COOKING TIME: 30 MINUTES

NOTE: The rice must absorb the stock between each addition — the whole process will take about 20 minutes. If you don't have time to make your own stock, you can buy fresh or frozen fish stock from delicatessens, some seafood outlets and most supermarkets.

TAGLIATELLE WITH GREEN OLIVES AND EGGPLANT

500 g (1 lb 2 oz) tagliatelle
175 g (6 oz/1 cup) green olives
1 large eggplant (aubergine)
2 tablespoons olive oil
2 garlic cloves, crushed
125 ml (4 fl oz/$^{1}/_{2}$ cup) lemon juice
2 tablespoons chopped flat-leaf (Italian) parsley
50 g (1$^{3}/_{4}$ oz/$^{1}/_{2}$ cup) freshly grated parmesan cheese

SERVES 4

Add the pasta to a large saucepan of rapidly boiling water and cook until *al dente*. Drain and return to the pan. While the pasta is cooking, chop the olives, removing the stones, and cut the eggplant into small cubes.

Heat the oil in a heavy-based frying pan. Add the garlic and stir for 30 seconds. Add the eggplant and cook over medium heat, stirring frequently, for 6 minutes or until tender.

Add the olives, lemon juice and salt and pepper to the pan. Add the sauce to the pasta and toss. Serve in bowls, sprinkled with parsley and parmesan cheese.

PREPARATION TIME: 20 MINUTES   COOKING TIME: 20 MINUTES

NOTE: If you prefer, the eggplant can be salted to draw out any bitter juices. Sprinkle the cut eggplant liberally with salt and leave to stand for 30 minutes. Rinse well before using.

GNOCCHI CHEESE BAKE

500 g (1 lb 2 oz) fresh potato gnocchi
30 g (1 oz) butter
1 tablespoon chopped flat-leaf (Italian parsley)
100 g (3$^{1}/_{2}$ oz) fontina cheese, sliced
100 g (3$^{1}/_{2}$ oz) provolone cheese, sliced

SERVES 4

Preheat the oven to 200°C (400°F/Gas 6). Cook the gnocchi, in batches, in a large saucepan of boiling water for about 2 minutes, or until the gnocchi rise to the surface. Carefully remove from the pan with a slotted spoon and drain well.

Put the gnocchi in a lightly greased ovenproof dish. Scatter with the butter and parsley. Lay the fontina and provolone cheeses over the top of the gnocchi. Season with sea salt and cracked black pepper. Bake for 10 minutes, or until the cheese has melted.

PREPARATION TIME: 10 MINUTES   COOKING TIME: 15 MINUTES

SUPPLI

750 ml (26 fl oz/3 cups) chicken stock
60 g (2¼ oz) butter
1 small onion, finely chopped
360 g (12¾ oz/1⅔ cups) risotto rice
125 ml (4 fl oz/½ cup) dry white wine
pinch powdered saffron
50 g (1¾ oz) parmesan cheese, grated
2 eggs, lightly beaten
100 g (3½ oz) mozzarella cheese
100 g (3½ oz/1 cup) dry breadcrumbs
oil, for deep-frying

MAKES 30

Put the stock in a saucepan and bring to the boil. Reduce the heat and maintain at simmering point.

Heat the butter in a large heavy-based frying pan. Add the onion and cook for 2–3 minutes, until softened but not brown. Add the rice and stir for a further 2–3 minutes, or until well coated with butter and onion.

Add the combined wine and saffron to the rice and stir until all the wine is absorbed. Add 125 ml (4 fl oz/½ cup) stock and stir continuously until absorbed, then continue adding the stock a little at a time, stirring, until 125 ml (4 fl oz/½ cup) stock remains. Add the remaining stock and stir, then cover with a tight-fitting lid. Reduce the heat to very low and cook for 10–15 minutes, until the rice is tender. Allow to cool.

Gently stir through the parmesan and eggs, and season to taste. Cut the mozzarella cheese into 30 small cubes. With wet hands, form the rice mixture into 30 walnut-sized balls. Push a cube of mozzarella into the centre of each ball and mould the rice around it.

Coat each ball with breadcrumbs. Chill for at least 1 hour to firm. Fill a deep heavy-based frying pan one-third full of oil and heat to 180°C (350°F), or until a cube of bread dropped into the oil browns in 15 seconds. Fry 3–4 balls at a time for 4–5 minutes, or until golden brown. Drain on crumpled paper towels. Serve hot.

PREPARATION TIME: 40 MINUTES +   COOKING TIME: 1 HOUR

NOTES: The full name is Suppli al Telefono. Serve hot, so that when bitten into, the cheese filling pulls out into long thin strands like telephone wires.

Cover and refrigerate for up to 3 days. Reheat in a warm oven for 15 minutes.

BAKED CANNELLONI MILANESE

500 g (1 lb 2 oz) minced (ground) pork and veal
50 g (1³/4 oz/1/2 cup) dry breadcrumbs
2 eggs, beaten
1 teaspoon dried oregano
100 g (3¹/2 oz/1 cup) freshly grated parmesan cheese
12–15 instant cannelloni tubes
375 g (13 oz) fresh ricotta cheese
60 g (2¹/4 oz/1/2 cup) freshly grated cheddar cheese

TOMATO SAUCE
425 ml (15 fl oz) tinned tomato passata (puréed tomatoes)
425 g (15 oz) tinned crushed tomatoes
2 garlic cloves, crushed
3 tablespoons chopped basil

SERVES 4

Preheat the oven to 180°C (350°F/Gas 4). Lightly grease a rectangular casserole dish.

In a bowl, combine the pork and veal, breadcrumbs, egg, oregano and half the parmesan, and season to taste. Use a teaspoon to stuff the cannelloni tubes with the mixture. Set aside.

To make the tomato sauce, bring the tomato passata, tomato and garlic to the boil in a saucepan. Reduce the heat and simmer for 15 minutes. Add the basil and pepper, to taste, and stir well.

Spoon half the tomato sauce over the base of the prepared dish. Arrange the stuffed cannelloni tubes on top. Cover with the remaining sauce. Spread with ricotta cheese. Sprinkle with the combined remaining parmesan and cheddar cheeses. Bake, covered with foil, for 1 hour. Uncover and bake for another 15 minutes, or until golden. Cut into squares to serve.

PREPARATION TIME: 40 MINUTES   COOKING TIME: 1 HOUR 35 MINUTES

FARFALLE WITH PEAS

500 g (1 lb 2 oz) farfalle
235 g (8¹/2 oz/1¹/2 cups) frozen baby peas
8 thin pancetta slices
60 g (2¹/4 oz) butter
2 tablespoons shredded basil
2 tablespoons shredded mint

SERVES 4

Cook the farfalle in a large saucepan of rapidly boiling salted water until *al dente*. Drain and return to the pan.

Meanwhile, steam or lightly boil the baby peas until just tender and drain.

Chop the pancetta and cook in the butter over medium heat for 2 minutes.

Toss the butter and pancetta mixture through the pasta with the peas, basil and mint. Season with cracked black pepper and serve.

PREPARATION TIME: 10 MINUTES   COOKING TIME: 20 MINUTES

GIANT CONCHIGLIE WITH RICOTTA AND ROCKET

40 giant conchiglie (shell pasta)

FILLING
500 g (1 lb 2 oz) ricotta cheese
100 g (3½ oz/1 cup) grated parmesan cheese
150 g (5½ oz) rocket (arugula), finely shredded
1 egg, lightly beaten
185 g (6½ oz) marinated globe artichokes, finely chopped
80 g (2¾ oz) sun-dried (sun-blushed) tomatoes, finely chopped
95 g (3¼ oz) sun-dried (sun-blushed) capsicum (pepper), finely chopped

CHEESE SAUCE
60 g (2¼ oz) butter
30 g (1 oz/¼ cup) plain (all-purpose) flour
750 ml (26 fl oz/3 cups) milk
100 g (3½ oz) gruyère cheese, grated
2 tablespoons chopped basil

600 ml (21 fl oz) bottled pasta sauce
2 tablespoons oregano, chopped
2 tablespoons basil

SERVES 6

Cook the giant conchiglie in a large saucepan of rapidly boiling salted water until *al dente*. Drain and arrange the shells on two non-stick baking trays to prevent them sticking together. Cover lightly with plastic wrap.

To make the filling, combine all the ingredients in a large bowl. Spoon the filling into the shells, taking care not to overfill them or they will split.

To make the cheese sauce, melt the butter in a small saucepan over low heat. Add the flour and stir for 1 minute, or until golden and smooth. Remove from the heat and gradually stir in the milk. Return to the heat and stir constantly until the sauce boils and begins to thicken. Simmer for a further minute. Remove from the heat and stir in the gruyère cheese with the basil and season to taste.

Preheat the oven to 180°C (350°F/Gas 4). Spread 250 ml (9 fl oz/1 cup) of the cheese sauce over the base of a 3 litre (104 fl oz/12-cup) capacity ovenproof dish. Arrange the filled conchiglie over the sauce, top with the remaining sauce and bake for 30 minutes, or until the sauce is golden.

Pour the bottled pasta sauce in a saucepan and add the oregano. Cook over medium heat for 5 minutes, or until heated through. To serve, divide the sauce among the warmed serving plates, top with the conchiglie and sprinkle with the basil leaves.

PREPARATION TIME: 50 MINUTES   COOKING TIME: 1 HOUR

RUOTE WITH LEMON, OLIVES AND BACON

500 g (1 lb 2 oz) ruote (see note)
6 bacon slices
125 g (4½ oz/1 cup) black olives, sliced
80 ml (2½ fl oz/⅓ cup) lemon juice
2 teaspoons finely grated lemon zest
80 ml (2½ fl oz/⅓ cup) olive oil
4 tablespoons chopped flat-leaf (Italian) parsley

SERVES 4

Cook the ruote in a large saucepan of rapidly boiling salted water until *al dente*. Drain and return to the pan.

While the pasta is cooking, discard the bacon rind and cut the bacon into thin strips. Cook in a frying pan until lightly browned.

In a bowl, combine the black olives, lemon juice, lemon zest, olive oil, chopped parsley and the bacon. Gently toss the olive and bacon mixture through the pasta until it is evenly distributed. Serve with freshly ground black pepper, to taste.

PREPARATION TIME: 10 MINUTES   COOKING TIME: 15 MINUTES

NOTE: Ruote is a pasta resembling wagon wheels. Small chunks of sauce are trapped between the spokes.

ARTICHOKE, EGG AND SORREL PASTA

500 g (1 lb 2 oz) conchiglie (shell pasta)
2 tablespoons oil
3 garlic cloves, crushed
315 g (11 oz) marinated artichoke hearts, halved
3 tablespoons chopped flat-leaf (Italian) parsley
165 g (5¾ oz) sorrel leaves, roughly chopped
4 hard-boiled eggs, chopped
parmesan cheese shavings, to serve

SERVES 4

Cook the conchiglie in a large saucepan of rapidly boiling salted water until *al dente*. Drain and keep warm.

While the pasta is cooking, heat the oil in a frying pan, add the garlic and cook over medium heat until golden. Add the artichoke hearts and chopped parsley and cook over low heat for 5 minutes, or until the artichoke hearts are heated through.

Transfer the pasta to a large bowl. Add the sorrel leaves, egg and artichoke hearts and toss to combine. Serve immediately, topped with shavings of parmesan and cracked black pepper to taste.

PREPARATION TIME: 15 MINUTES   COOKING TIME: 20 MINUTES

SPAGHETTI WITH SARDINES, FENNEL AND TOMATO

3 roma (plum) tomatoes
80 ml (2^1/2 fl oz/^{1}/3 cup) olive oil
3 garlic cloves, crushed
80 g (2^3/4 oz/1 cup) fresh white breadcrumbs
1 red onion, thinly sliced
1 fennel bulb, quartered and thinly sliced
40 g (1^1/2 oz/^{1}/4 cup) raisins
40 g (1^1/2 oz/^{1}/4 cup) pine nuts, toasted
4 anchovy fillets, chopped
125 ml (4 fl oz/^{1}/2 cup) dry white wine
1 tablespoon tomato paste (concentrated purée)
4 tablespoons finely chopped flat-leaf (Italian) parsley
350 g (12 oz) butterflied sardine fillets
500 g (1 lb 2 oz) spaghetti

SERVES 4–6

Score a cross in the base of each tomato. Place the tomatoes in a bowl of boiling water for 10 seconds, then plunge into cold water and peel the skin away from the cross. Cut the tomatoes in half and scoop out the seeds. Roughly chop the tomato flesh.

Heat 1 tablespoon of the oil in a large frying pan over medium heat. Add 1 garlic clove and the breadcrumbs and stir for about 5 minutes, until golden and crisp. Transfer to a plate.

Heat the remaining oil in the same pan and cook the onion, fennel and remaining garlic for 8 minutes, or until soft. Add the tomato, raisins, pine nuts and anchovies and cook for a further 3 minutes. Add the wine, tomato paste and 125 ml (4 fl oz/^{1}/2 cup) water. Simmer for 10 minutes, or until the mixture thickens slightly. Stir in the parsley and set aside.

Pat the sardines dry with paper towels. Cook the sardines in batches in a lightly greased frying pan over medium heat for 1 minute, or until cooked through. Take care not to overcook or they will break up. Set aside.

Cook the pasta in a large saucepan of rapidly boiling salted water until *al dente*. Drain and return to the pan.

Stir the sauce through the pasta until the pasta is well coated and the sauce evenly distributed. Add the sardines and half the breadcrumbs and toss gently. Sprinkle the remaining breadcrumbs over the top and serve immediately.

PREPARATION TIME: 30 MINUTES   COOKING TIME: 45 MINUTES

TUSCAN WARM PASTA SALAD

500 g (1 lb 2 oz) rigatoni
80 ml (2½ fl oz/⅓ cup) olive oil
1 garlic clove, crushed
1 tablespoon balsamic vinegar
425 g (15 oz) tinned artichoke hearts,
drained and quartered
8 thin prosciutto slices, chopped
80 g (2¾ oz/½ cup) sun-dried
(sun-blushed) tomatoes in oil,
drained and thinly sliced
15 g (½ oz/¼ cup) basil, shredded
70 g (2½ oz) rocket (arugula) leaves,
washed and drained well
40 g (1½ oz/¼ cup) pine nuts, toasted
45 g (1½ oz/¼ cup) black Italian olives

SERVES 6

Add the rigatoni to a large saucepan of rapidly boiling water and cook until *al dente*. Drain the pasta thoroughly and transfer to a large bowl.

While the pasta is cooking, whisk together the oil, garlic and balsamic vinegar. Toss the dressing through the hot pasta. Allow the pasta to cool slightly. Add the artichoke hearts, prosciutto, sun-dried tomato, basil, rocket, pine nuts and olives.

Toss all the ingredients together until well combined. Season to taste.

PREPARATION TIME: 15 MINUTES   COOKING TIME: 15 MINUTES

NOTE: To toast the pine nuts, cook in a dry frying pan over medium heat for 1–2 minutes, until lightly golden. Allow to cool.

GRILLED CAPSICUM AND ANCHOVY SALAD

500 g (1 lb 2 oz) penne
2 large red capsicums (peppers)
1 small red onion, finely chopped
1 large handful flat-leaf (Italian)
parsley
2–3 anchovy fillets, whole or chopped
60 ml (2 fl oz/¼ cup) olive oil
2 tablespoons lemon juice

SERVES 6

Cook the pasta in a large saucepan of rapidly boiling salted water until *al dente*. Drain, rinse under cold water and drain again.

Cut the capsicums in half and remove the seeds and membrane. Place, skin side up, under a hot grill (broiler) and cook for 8 minutes, or until the skin is black and blistered. Remove from the heat and cover with a damp tea towel (dish towel). When cool, peel away the skin and cut the flesh into thin strips.

In a large salad bowl, combine the pasta, capsicum strips, onion, parsley, anchovies, oil and lemon juice, and season to taste. Toss until well combined and serve immediately.

PREPARATION TIME: 15 MINUTES   COOKING TIME: 25 MINUTES

LEMON AND HERB RISOTTO WITH FRIED MUSHROOMS

1 litre (35 fl oz/4 cups) chicken or vegetable stock
pinch saffron threads
2 tablespoons olive oil
2 leeks, thinly sliced
2 garlic cloves, crushed
440 g (15½ oz/2 cups) risotto rice
2–3 teaspoons finely grated lemon zest
2 tablespoons lemon juice
2 tablespoons chopped flat-leaf (Italian) parsley
2 tablespoons snipped chives
2 tablespoons chopped oregano
75 g (2½ oz/¾ cup) freshly grated parmesan cheese
100 g (3½ oz) mascarpone cheese
30 g (1 oz) butter
1 tablespoon olive oil
200 g (7 oz) small flat mushrooms, cut into thick slices
1 tablespoon balsamic vinegar

SERVES 4

Pour the stock into a saucepan and add the saffron threads. Bring to the boil, then reduce the heat, cover and keep at a low simmer.

Heat the olive oil in a large saucepan over medium heat. Add the leek, cook for 5 minutes, then add the garlic and cook for a further 5 minutes, or until golden. Add the rice and stir until well coated. Add half the lemon zest and half the juice, then add 125 ml (4 fl oz/½ cup) of the hot stock. Stir constantly over medium heat until all the liquid has been absorbed. Continue adding more liquid, 125 ml (4 fl oz/½ cup) at a time until all the liquid is absorbed and the rice is tender and creamy. (You may not need to use all the stock, or you may need a little extra — every risotto will be slightly different.)

Remove the pan from the heat. Stir in the herbs, parmesan, mascarpone and the remaining lemon zest and lemon juice. Cover and keep warm.

To cook the mushrooms, melt the butter and olive oil in a large frying pan, add the mushroom slices and vinegar and cook, stirring, over high heat for 5–7 minutes, or until the mushrooms are tender and all the liquid has been absorbed.

Serve the risotto in large bowls topped with the mushrooms.

PREPARATION TIME: 30 MINUTES   COOKING TIME: 50 MINUTES

SPAGHETTI WITH CREAMY GARLIC MUSSELS

500 g (1 lb 2 oz) spaghetti
1.5 kg (3 lb 5 oz) mussels
2 tablespoons olive oil
2 garlic cloves, crushed
125 ml (4 fl oz/$\frac{1}{2}$ cup) dry white wine
250 ml (9 fl oz/1 cup) pouring (whipping) cream
2 tablespoons chopped basil

SERVES 4

Cook the spaghetti in a large saucepan of rapidly boiling salted water until *al dente*. Drain.

Meanwhile, scrub the mussels with a stiff brush and pull out the hairy beards. Discard any broken mussels, or open ones that don't close when tapped on the bench. Rinse well.

Heat the oil in a large saucepan. Add the garlic and stir over low heat for 30 seconds. Add the wine and mussels. Simmer, covered, for 5 minutes. Remove the mussels, discarding any that don't open, and set aside.

Add the cream and basil to the pan and season to taste. Simmer for 2 minutes, stirring. Serve the sauce and mussels over the spaghetti.

PREPARATION TIME: 20 MINUTES   COOKING TIME: 15 MINUTES

BUCATINI ALLA NORMA

185 ml (6 fl oz/$\frac{3}{4}$ cup) olive oil
1 onion, finely chopped
2 garlic cloves, crushed
800 g (1 lb 12 oz) tinned crushed tomatoes
1 large eggplant (aubergine)
1 handful basil, torn
400 g (14 oz) bucatini
60 g (2$\frac{1}{4}$ oz/$\frac{1}{2}$ cup) ricotta salata, crumbled
50 g (1$\frac{3}{4}$ oz/$\frac{1}{2}$ cup) grated pecorino or parmesan cheese
1 tablespoon extra virgin olive oil

SERVES 4–6

Heat 2 tablespoons of the oil in a heavy-based frying pan and cook the onion over medium heat for 5 minutes, or until softened. Add the garlic to the pan and cook for a further 30 seconds. Add the tomato and season to taste. Reduce the heat and cook for 20–25 minutes, or until the sauce has thickened and reduced.

Cut the eggplant lengthways into 5 mm ($\frac{1}{4}$ inch) thick slices. Heat the remaining olive oil in a large heavy-based frying pan. When the oil is hot, add the eggplant slices a few at a time and cook for 3–5 minutes, or until lightly browned on both sides. Remove and drain well on paper towels. Cut each slice of eggplant into 3 pieces and add to the tomato sauce with the torn basil. Stir and keep warm over very low heat.

Cook the bucatini in a large saucepan of rapidly boiling salted water until *al dente*. Drain well and add to the tomato sauce with half each of the ricotta and pecorino. Toss well and serve sprinkled with the remaining cheeses. Drizzle with the extra virgin olive oil.

PREPARATION TIME: 15 MINUTES   COOKING TIME: 50 MINUTES

Spaghetti with creamy garlic mussels

PUMPKIN AND HERB RAVIOLI

500 g (1 lb 2 oz) pumpkin (winter squash),
peeled and cut into chunks
220 g (7³/4 oz/1³/4 cups) plain
(all-purpose) flour
3 eggs, lightly beaten
¹/4 teaspoon freshly grated nutmeg
15 sage leaves
15 flat-leaf (Italian) parsley leaves
125 g (4¹/2 oz) butter, melted
60 g (2¹/4 oz) freshly grated parmesan
cheese

SERVES 6

Preheat the oven to 180°C (350°F/Gas 4). Place the pumpkin on an oiled baking tray and bake for 1 hour or until tender, then allow to cool. Remove the skin. Place the flour and eggs in a food processor. Process for 30 seconds, or until the mixture forms a dough. Transfer to a lightly floured surface and knead for 3 minutes, or until the dough is smooth and elastic. Cover with a clean cloth and set aside for 30 minutes.

Place the pumpkin in a bowl with the nutmeg and mash with a fork. Roll out half the dough to form a rectangle about 2 mm (¹/16 inch) thick. Roll out the remaining half to form a rectangle slightly larger than the first.

On the first rectangle of dough, place heaped teaspoonsful of the pumpkin mixture in straight rows, at intervals about 5 cm (2 inches) apart. Flatten each pumpkin mound slightly; place one whole sage or parsley leaf on top of each spoonful of pumpkin mixture.

Brush lightly between the mounds of filling with water. Place the second sheet of dough on top and then press down gently between the pumpkin mounds to seal. Cut into squares with a knife or a fluted cutter. Bring a large saucepan of water to the boil and drop in the ravioli a few at a time. Cook for 4 minutes, or until just tender. Drain well. Serve the ravioli sprinkled with salt and pepper and tossed with melted butter and parmesan cheese.

PREPARATION TIME: 50 MINUTES +   COOKING TIME: 1 HOUR 15 MINUTES

NOTE: Ravioli can be made several hours in advance. Refrigerate in layers between sheets of baking paper to prevent them sticking together. Cook just before serving.

RISOTTO PRIMAVERA

1.5 litres (52 fl oz/6 cups) chicken or
vegetable stock
2 tablespoons olive oil
70 g (2^1/2 oz) butter
1 large onion, finely chopped
1 carrot, finely diced
2 garlic cloves, crushed
440 g (15^1/2 oz/2 cups) risotto rice
200 g (7 oz) thin asparagus, cut into
2 cm (^{3}/4 inch) pieces
2 small zucchini (courgettes), thinly sliced
115 g (4 oz/^{3}/4 cup) fresh peas
15 g (^{1}/2 oz/^{1}/2 cup) chopped flat-leaf
(Italian) parsley
50 g (1^3/4 oz/^{1}/2 cup) freshly grated
parmesan cheese

SERVES 6

Pour the stock into a saucepan and bring to the boil. Reduce the heat, cover with a lid and keep at a low simmer.

Heat the oil and half the butter in a large heavy-based saucepan over medium heat. Add the onion and carrot and stir for 5 minutes. Add the garlic and cook, stirring, for 2 minutes, or until the onion is softened. Stir in the rice until well coated.

Add 125 ml (4 fl oz/^{1}/2 cup) of the hot stock. Stir constantly over medium heat until nearly all the liquid is absorbed. Continue adding the stock, 125 ml (4 fl oz/^{1}/2 cup) at a time, stirring. After 10 minutes, add the asparagus, zucchini and peas. Continue adding the remaining stock. Cook for a further 10–15 minutes, or until the rice is tender and creamy.

Remove from the heat and stir in the parsley, parmesan and remaining butter. Season to taste.

PREPARATION TIME: 15 MINUTES   COOKING TIME: 35 MINUTES

ASPARAGUS RISOTTO

1 kg (2 lb 4 oz) asparagus
500 ml (17 fl oz/2 cups) chicken stock
500 ml (17 fl oz/2 cups) vegetable stock
80 ml (2^1/2 fl oz/^{1}/3 cup) olive oil
1 small onion, finely chopped
360 g (12^3/4 oz/1^2/3 cups) risotto rice
75 g (2^1/2 oz/^{3}/4 cup) freshly grated
parmesan cheese
60 g (2^1/4 oz/^{1}/4 cup) thick
(double/heavy) cream

SERVES 4

Wash the asparagus and remove the woody ends. Separate the tender spear tips from the stems. Cook the asparagus stems in boiling water for 8 minutes, or until tender. Drain and put in a blender with the chicken and vegetable stocks. Blend for 1 minute, then scoop the mixture into a saucepan. Bring to the boil, reduce the heat, cover and keep at a low simmer. Cook the asparagus tips in boiling water for 1 minute, then drain and refresh in iced water so they stop cooking.

Heat the olive oil in a large saucepan. Cook the onion until softened. Stir in the rice. Add 125 ml (4 fl oz/^{1}/2 cup) of the hot stock and stir over medium heat until all the liquid is absorbed. Continue adding more stock, 125 ml (4 fl oz/^{1}/2 cup) at a time until all the liquid is absorbed and the rice is tender and creamy. Remove from the heat, then stir in the parmesan, cream and asparagus tips. Season to taste.

PREPARATION TIME: 20 MINUTES   COOKING TIME: 35 MINUTES

RIGATONI WITH ITALIAN-STYLE OXTAIL SAUCE

2 tablespoons olive oil
1.5 kg (3 lb 5 oz) oxtail, jointed
2 large onions, sliced
4 garlic cloves, chopped
2 celery stalks, sliced
2 carrots, thinly sliced
2 large rosemary sprigs
60 ml (2 fl oz/¼ cup) red wine
60 ml (2 fl oz/¼ cup) tomato paste
(concentrated purée)
4 tomatoes, peeled and chopped
1.5 litres (52 fl oz/6 cups) beef stock
500 g (1 lb 2 oz) rigatoni

SERVES 4

Heat the oil in a large heavy-based saucepan. Brown the oxtail, remove from the pan and set aside. Add the onion, garlic, celery and carrot to the pan and stir for 3–4 minutes, or until the onion is lightly browned.

Return the oxtail to the pan and add the rosemary and red wine. Cover and cook for 10 minutes, shaking the pan occasionally to prevent the meat from sticking to the bottom. Add the tomato paste and chopped tomato to the pan with 500 ml (17 fl oz/2 cups) of the beef stock and simmer, uncovered, for 30 minutes, stirring the mixture occasionally.

Add another 500 ml (17 fl oz/2 cups) of beef stock to the pan and cook for 30 minutes. Add 250 ml (9 fl oz/1 cup) of stock and cook for 30 minutes. Finally, add the remaining stock and cook until the oxtail is tender and the meat is falling from the bone. The liquid should have reduced to produce a thick sauce.

Just before the meat is cooked, cook the pasta in a large saucepan of rapidly boiling salted water until *al dente*. Serve the meat and sauce over the hot pasta.

PREPARATION TIME: 25 MINUTES   COOKING TIME: 2 HOURS

NOTE: For a different flavour, you can add 250 g (9 oz) bacon to the cooked onion, garlic and vegetables.

MEAT AND FISH

SEAFOOD SALAD

500 g (1 lb 2 oz) small squid
1 kg (2 lb 4 oz) large clams
1 kg (2 lb 4 oz) mussels
4 tablespoons chopped flat-leaf (Italian)
parsley (reserve the stalks), plus extra,
to garnish
500 g (1 lb 2 oz) raw prawns (shrimp),
peeled, deveined, tails intact
2 tablespoons lemon juice
80 ml (2^1/$_2$ fl oz/^{1}/$_3$ cup) olive oil
1 garlic clove, crushed

SERVES 4

To clean the squid, gently pull the tentacles away from the tube (the intestines should come away at the same time). Remove the intestines from the tentacles by cutting under the eyes, then remove the beak if it remains in the centre of the tentacles by using your fingers to push up the centre. Pull away the quill (the transparent cartilage) from inside the body and remove. Remove and discard any white membrane. Under cold running water pull away the skin from the hood. Rinse, then slice into 7 mm (^{3}/$_8$ inch) rings.

Scrub the clams and mussels with a stiff brush and pull out the hairy beards. Discard any broken mussels, or open ones that don't close when tapped on the bench. Rinse well. Fill a wide shallow frying pan with 1 cm (^{1}/$_2$ inch) water, add the parsley stalks, cover the pan and bring the water to simmering point. Add the clams and mussels in batches, being careful not to overcrowd the pan. Cover and steam over high heat for 2–3 minutes, or until the shells begin to open. Remove with a slotted spoon and place in a colander over a bowl. Return any drained juices to the pan before cooking the next batch. Continue until all the clams and mussels are cooked. Reserve the cooking liquid. Allow the clams and mussels to cool before removing them from the shells. Discard any unopened ones.

Add 1 litre (35 fl oz/4 cups) water to the pan with the cooking liquid. Bring to the boil, then add the prawns and cook for 3–4 minutes, or until the water returns to the boil. Remove with a slotted spoon and drain in a colander. Add the squid and cook for 30–40 seconds, until the flesh becomes white and opaque. Remove immediately and drain.

Whisk the lemon juice, oil and garlic in a bowl, then season. Pour over the seafood with the parsley, then toss. Adjust the seasoning if necessary. Marinate for 30–40 minutes to allow the flavours to develop. Sprinkle with extra parsley. Serve with crusty bread.

PREPARATION TIME: 45 MINUTES +   COOKING TIME: 25 MINUTES

ROMAN LAMB

60 ml (2 fl oz/¼ cup) olive oil
1 kg (2 lb 4 oz) spring lamb, cut into
2 cm (¾ inch) cubes
2 garlic cloves, crushed
6 sage leaves
1 rosemary sprig
1 tablespoon plain (all-purpose) flour
125 ml (4 fl oz/½ cup) white wine vinegar
6 anchovy fillets

SERVES 4–6

Heat the oil in a heavy-based frying pan and cook the meat in batches over medium heat for 3–4 minutes, until browned on all sides.

Return all the meat to the pan and add the garlic, sage and rosemary. Season, combine well and cook for 1 minute.

Dust the meat with the flour using a fine sieve, then cook for a further 1 minute. Add the vinegar and simmer for 30 seconds, then add 250 ml (9 fl oz/1 cup) water. Bring to a gentle simmer, lower the heat and cover, leaving the lid partially askew. Cook for 50–60 minutes, or until the meat is tender, stirring occasionally and adding a little more water if necessary.

When the lamb is almost cooked, mash the anchovies using a mortar and pestle with 1 tablespoon of the cooking liquid, until a paste is formed. Add to the lamb and cook, uncovered, for another 2 minutes.

PREPARATION TIME: 15 MINUTES   COOKING TIME: 1 HOUR 20 MINUTES

NOTE: This dish is best served immediately but can be prepared in advance. The anchovies should be added at the last moment or they will overpower the delicate flavour of the lamb.

SWEET AND SOUR LIVER

40 g (1½ oz) butter
80 ml (2½ fl oz/⅓ cup) olive oil
600 g (1 lb 5 oz) calves' livers, cut into long thin slices
80 g (2¾ oz/1 cup) fresh white breadcrumbs
1 tablespoon sugar
2 garlic cloves, crushed
60 ml (2 fl oz/¼ cup) red wine vinegar
1 tablespoon chopped flat-leaf (Italian) parsley

SERVES 4

Heat the butter and half the oil in a heavy-based frying pan over medium heat. Coat the liver in breadcrumbs, pressing them on firmly with your hands. Shake off the excess and place in the pan when the butter begins to foam. Cook on each side for 1 minute, or until the crust is brown and crisp. Remove from the pan and keep warm.

Add the remaining oil to the frying pan and cook the sugar and garlic over low heat until golden. Add the vinegar and cook for 30 seconds, or until almost evaporated. Add the parsley and pour over the liver. Serve hot or at room temperature.

PREPARATION TIME: 10 MINUTES   COOKING TIME: 10 MINUTES

Abbacchio (roman lamb)

ZUPPA DI COZZE

200 g (7 oz) ripe tomatoes
1 kg (2 lb 4 oz) black mussels
2 tablespoons olive oil
40 g (1¹/₂ oz) butter
1 leek, finely chopped
3 garlic cloves, crushed
pinch saffron threads
1 tablespoon finely chopped flat-leaf
(Italian) parsley
1 small red chilli, finely chopped
170 ml (5¹/₂ fl oz/²/₃ cup) dry white wine

SERVES 6

Score a cross in the base of each tomato. Place in a heatproof bowl and cover with boiling water. Leave for 30 seconds, transfer to cold water, drain and peel away the skin from the cross. Cut the tomatoes in half, scoop out the seeds and finely chop the flesh.

Scrub the mussels with a stiff brush and pull out the hairy beards. Discard any broken mussels, or open ones that don't close when tapped on the bench. Rinse well.

Heat the oil and butter in a large saucepan and cook the leek and garlic over low heat until the leek is soft but not brown. Add the saffron, parsley and chilli and cook, stirring, for 1–2 minutes. Increase the heat and add the wine. Bring to the boil and cook for 1–2 minutes, then add the chopped tomato and 250 ml (9 fl oz/1 cup) water. Cover and simmer for 20 minutes.

Add the mussels to the pan and cook, covered, until they are opened. After 4-5 minutes, discard any unopened mussels. So the soup is not too crowded with shells, remove one third of the remaining mussels, remove the mussel meat and add to the soup. Discard the empty shells. Season to taste. Serve immediately with crusty bread.

PREPARATION TIME: 25 MINUTES   COOKING TIME: 35 MINUTES

PORK CHOPS IN MARSALA

4 pork loin chops
2 tablespoons olive oil
125 ml (4 fl oz/½ cup) Marsala
2 teaspoons grated orange zest
60 ml (2 fl oz/¼ cup) orange juice
3 tablespoons chopped flat-leaf (Italian)
parsley

SERVES 4

Pat dry the chops and season well. Heat the olive oil in a heavy-based frying pan over medium heat and cook the chops on both sides for 5 minutes each side, or until brown and cooked. Add the Marsala, orange zest and juice and cook for 4–5 minutes, or until the sauce has reduced and thickened. Add the parsley and serve.

PREPARATION TIME: 10 MINUTES   COOKING TIME: 15 MINUTES

GRILLED SQUID WITH SALSA VERDE

1 kg (2 lb 4 oz) squid
250 ml (9 fl oz/1 cup) olive oil
2 tablespoons lemon juice
2 garlic cloves, crushed
2 tablespoons chopped oregano
2 tablespoons chopped flat-leaf (Italian)
parsley, to serve
6 lemon wedges, to serve

SALSA VERDE
4 anchovy fillets, drained
1 tablespoon capers
1 garlic clove, crushed
3 tablespoons chopped flat-leaf (Italian)
parsley
1 small handful basil
1 small handful mint
2 teaspoons red wine vinegar
60 ml (2 fl oz/¼ cup) extra virgin olive oil
1 teaspoon dijon mustard

SERVES 6

To clean the squid, gently pull the tentacles away from the tube (the intestines should come away at the same time). Remove the intestines from the tentacles by cutting under the eyes, then remove the beak if it remains in the centre of the tentacles by using your fingers to push up the centre. Pull away the quill (the transparent cartilage) from inside the body and remove. Remove and discard any white membrane. Under cold running water pull away the skin from the hood. Cut into 1 cm (½ inch) rings and place in the bowl with the tentacles. Add the oil, lemon juice, garlic and oregano to the bowl, and toss to coat the squid. Leave to marinate for 30 minutes.

To make the salsa verde, put the anchovies, capers, garlic, parsley, basil and mint in a food processor and chop in short bursts until roughly blended. Transfer to a bowl and stir in the vinegar. Slowly mix in the oil, then the mustard. Season.

Heat a barbecue or chargrill pan until hot. Drain the squid rings and cook them in batches for 1–2 minutes each side.

Season the squid rings and sprinkle with the parsley. Serve with the salsa verde and lemon wedges.

PREPARATION TIME: 10 MINUTES +   COOKING TIME: 10 MINUTES

Pork chops in Marsala

ROASTED ROSEMARY CHICKEN

1.5–1.8 kg (3 lb 5 oz–4 lb) chicken
6 large rosemary sprigs
4 garlic cloves
60 ml (2 fl oz/¼ cup) olive oil

SERVES 4

Preheat the oven to 220°C (425°F/Gas 7). Wipe the chicken inside and out and pat dry with paper towels. Season the chicken cavity and place four rosemary sprigs and the garlic cloves inside.

Rub the outside of the chicken with 1 tablespoon of the oil, season and place the chicken on its side in a roasting tin. Put the remaining rosemary sprigs in the tin and drizzle the remaining oil around the tin.

Place the tin on the middle shelf in the oven. After 20 minutes, turn the chicken onto the other side, baste with the juices and cook for a further 20 minutes. Turn the chicken, breast side up, baste again and cook for a further 15 minutes, or until the juices between the body and thigh run clear when pierced with a knife. Transfer the chicken to a warm serving dish and set aside for at least 10 minutes before carving.

Meanwhile, pour off most of the fat from the roasting tin and return the tin to the stovetop over high heat. Add 2 tablespoons water and, using a wooden spoon, scrape the base of the pan to loosen the residue. Check the seasoning and pour over the chicken to serve.

PREPARATION TIME: 15 MINUTES +   COOKING TIME: 1 HOUR

SALTIMBOCCA

4 thin veal steaks
2 garlic cloves, crushed
4 prosciutto slices
4 sage leaves
30 g (1 oz) butter
170 ml (5½ fl oz/⅔ cup) Marsala

SERVES 4

Trim the meat of excess fat and sinew and flatten each steak to 5 mm (¼ inch) thick. Nick the edges to prevent curling and pat the meat dry with paper towels. Combine the garlic with ¼ teaspoon salt and ½ teaspoon ground black pepper and rub some of the mixture over one side of each veal steak. Place a slice of prosciutto on each and top with a sage leaf. The prosciutto should cover the veal completely but not overlap the edge.

Melt the butter in a large heavy-based frying pan, add the veal, prosciutto side up, and cook over heat for 5 minutes, or until the underside is golden brown. Do not turn the veal. Add the Marsala, without wetting the top of the veal. Reduce the heat and simmer very slowly for 10 minutes. Transfer the veal to warm serving plates. Boil the sauce for 2–3 minutes, or until syrupy, then spoon it over the veal.

PREPARATION TIME: 15 MINUTES   COOKING TIME: 20 MINUTES

MEATBALLS

250 g (9 oz) minced (ground) lean beef
1 small onion, grated
1 garlic clove, crushed
40 g (1½ oz/½ cup) fresh white breadcrumbs
40 g (1½ oz) pitted black olives, chopped
1 teaspoon dried oregano
1 tablespoon finely chopped flat-leaf (Italian) parsley
oil, for pan-frying

MAKES ABOUT 25

Combine the beef, onion, garlic, breadcrumbs, olives, oregano, parsley and salt and black pepper, to taste. Mix together thoroughly.

Form teaspoons of the mixture into balls. This is easier if you roll them with wet hands. Heat a little oil in a frying pan and cook the meatballs in batches until well browned and cooked through.

PREPARATION TIME: 25 MINUTES   COOKING TIME: 20 MINUTES

NOTE: You can prepare the meatballs, cover and refrigerate, then cook when you are ready, or cook them in advance and reheat them, lightly covered with foil, in a 160°C (315°F/Gas 2–3) oven. They can also be cooked and frozen, then reheated.

OCTOPUS IN RED WINE

1 kg (2 lb 4 oz) baby octopus
2 tablespoons olive oil
175 g (6 oz) baby onions
80 ml (2½ fl oz/⅓ cup) red wine vinegar
185 ml (6 fl oz/¾ cup) dry red wine
1 ripe tomato, grated
1 bay leaf
1 teaspoon dried oregano

SERVES 4

To clean the octopus, using a small knife, carefully cut between the head and tentacles of the octopus, just below the eyes. Grasp the body of the octopus and push the beak out and up through the centre of the tentacles with your finger. Cut the eyes from the head of the octopus by slicing a small disc off with a sharp knife. Discard the eyes section. To clean the octopus head, carefully slit through one side, avoiding the ink sac and scrape out any gut from inside. Rinse under running water to remove any remaining grit. Cut the tentacles into sets of four or two, depending on the size of the octopus.

Place the octopus in a large frying pan and cook over high heat in their own liquid for 15–20 minutes, or until dry. Add the oil and the onions, and toss over heat until well coated. Add the vinegar, wine, tomato, bay leaf, oregano, 250 ml (9 fl oz/1 cup) water and ½ teaspoon cracked black pepper, and bring to the boil. Reduce the heat to low and simmer for 1½–2 hours, or until the flesh is tender. If not yet tender, add a little more water and continue cooking. The liquid remaining in the pan should just coat the octopus like a sauce.

PREPARATION TIME: 45 MINUTES   COOKING TIME: 2 HOURS 20 MINUTES

NOTE: Young, small octopus are more tender than large ones. The octopus is closely related to squid and cuttlefish, so if you are unable to buy small octopus, you can use either of these.

RABBIT WITH ROSEMARY AND WHITE WINE

1 large rabbit (about 1.6 kg/3 lb 8 oz)

30 g (1 oz/¼ cup) seasoned flour

60 ml (2 fl oz/¼ cup) olive oil

2 onions, thinly sliced

1 large rosemary sprig

1 small sage sprig

2 garlic cloves, crushed

500 ml (17 fl oz/2 cups) dry white wine

400 g (14 oz) tinned chopped tomatoes

pinch cayenne pepper

125 ml (4 fl oz/½ cup) chicken stock

12 small black olives such as Niçoise or Ligurian (optional)

3 small rosemary sprigs, extra (optional)

Cut the rabbit into large pieces and dredge the pieces in the flour. Heat the oil in a large heavy-based saucepan over medium heat. Brown the rabbit pieces on all sides, then remove from the saucepan.

Reduce the heat and add the onion, rosemary and sage to the saucepan. Cook gently for 10 minutes, then stir in the garlic and return the rabbit to the saucepan.

Increase the heat to high, add the wine to the pan and cook for 1 minute. Stir in the tomato, the cayenne and half the stock. Reduce the heat, cover and simmer over low heat for about 1½ hours, or until the rabbit is tender. Halfway through cooking, check the sauce and if it seems too dry, add 60 ml (2 fl oz/¼ cup) water. Discard the herb sprigs. Season to taste. Garnish with the olives and extra rosemary, if desired.

SERVES 4   PREPARATION TIME: 25 MINUTES COOKING TIME: 2 HOURS

FISH CRUSTED WITH PARMESAN AND HERBS

4 x 200 g (7 oz) skinless firm white fish fillets, such as ling, snapper or perch

seasoned flour, for dusting

1 egg

1 tablespoon milk

50 g (1¾ oz/½ cup) dry breadcrumbs

2 tablespoons chopped dill

2 tablespoons chopped flat-leaf (Italian) parsley

35 g (1¼ oz/⅓ cup) freshly grated parmesan cheese

30 g (1 oz/⅓ cup) flaked almonds, lightly crushed

1 tablespoon olive oil

30 g (1 oz) butter

Lightly dust the fillets with seasoned flour. Whisk the egg with the milk.

Combine the breadcrumbs, dill, parsley, parmesan and almonds.

Dip the fillets into the egg, then coat with the breadcrumb mixture. Press on firmly.

Heat the oil and butter in a frying pan, add the fish and cook over medium heat on both sides until golden and cooked. Serve with tartare sauce.

PREPARATION TIME: 15 MINUTES   COOKING TIME: 20 MINUTES

SERVES 4

CHICKEN CACCIATORA

60 ml (2 fl oz/$\frac{1}{4}$ cup) olive oil
1 large onion, finely chopped
3 garlic cloves, crushed
150 g (5$\frac{1}{2}$ oz) pancetta, finely chopped
125 g (4$\frac{1}{2}$ oz) button mushrooms, thickly sliced
1 large chicken (at least 1.6 kg/3 lb 8 oz), cut into 8 pieces
80 ml (2$\frac{1}{2}$ fl oz/$\frac{1}{3}$ cup) dry vermouth or dry white wine
800 g (1 lb 12 oz) tinned chopped tomatoes
$\frac{1}{4}$ teaspoon soft brown sugar
$\frac{1}{4}$ teaspoon cayenne pepper
1 oregano sprig
1 thyme sprig
1 bay leaf

SERVES 4

Heat half the olive oil in a large flameproof casserole dish. Add the onion and garlic and cook for 6–8 minutes over low heat, stirring, until the onion is golden. Add the pancetta and mushrooms, increase the heat and cook, stirring, for 4–5 minutes. Transfer to a bowl.

Add the remaining oil to the casserole dish and brown the chicken pieces, a few at a time, over medium heat. Season as they brown. Spoon off the excess fat and return all the chicken to the casserole dish. Increase the heat, add the vermouth to the dish and cook until the liquid has almost evaporated.

Add the chopped tomato, brown sugar, cayenne pepper, oregano, thyme and bay leaf, and stir in 80 ml (2$\frac{1}{2}$ fl oz/$\frac{1}{3}$ cup) water. Bring to the boil, then stir in the reserved onion mixture. Reduce the heat, cover and simmer for 25 minutes, or until the chicken is tender but not falling off the bone.

If the liquid is too thin, remove the chicken from the casserole dish, increase the heat and boil until the liquid has thickened. Discard the sprigs of herbs and adjust the seasoning.

PREPARATION TIME: 15 MINUTES   COOKING TIME: 1 HOUR

FISH ROLLS

1 large ripe tomato
1 tablespoon drained capers, chopped
40 g (1¹/₂ oz) stuffed green olives, chopped
3 tablespoons chopped lemon thyme
30 g (1 oz) romano cheese, finely grated
2 teaspoons finely grated lemon zest
8 thin firm skinless white fish fillets, such as John dory, bream, perch, snapper
250 ml (9 fl oz/1 cup) dry white wine
2 tablespoons lemon juice
3 tablespoons lemon thyme
2 bay leaves

SERVES 4

Preheat the oven to 160°C (315°F/Gas 2–3). Score a cross in the base of the tomato. Place in a heatproof bowl and cover with boiling water. Leave for 30 seconds, then transfer to cold water and peel away the skin. Cut in half and scoop out the seeds. Roughly chop the flesh and mix with the capers, olives, thyme, cheese, lemon zest and ¹/₄ teaspoon freshly ground black pepper, in a small bowl.

Place the fillets, skinned side up, on a flat surface. Spread the tomato mixture evenly onto each fillet, then roll tightly and secure with a toothpick or skewer. Place in a single layer in a shallow casserole dish.

Pour the combined wine, lemon juice, thyme and bay leaves over the fish, cover and bake for 20 minutes, or until the fish is cooked and flakes easily when tested with a fork.

PREPARATION TIME: 25 MINUTES   COOKING TIME: 20 MINUTES

INVOLTINI OF SWORDFISH

1 kg (2 lb 4 oz) swordfish, skin removed, cut into four 4 x 5 cm (1¹/₂ x 2 inch) pieces
3 lemons
80 ml (2¹/₂ fl oz/¹/₃ cup) olive oil
1 small onion, chopped
3 garlic cloves, chopped
2 tablespoons chopped capers
2 tablespoons chopped Kalamata olives
35 g (1¹/₄ oz/¹/₃ cup) freshly grated parmesan cheese
120 g (4¹/₄ oz/1¹/₂ cups) fresh white breadcrumbs
2 tablespoons chopped flat-leaf (Italian) parsley
1 egg, lightly beaten
24 bay leaves
2 small white onions, quartered

SERVES 4

Cut each swordfish piece horizontally into four slices to give you 16 slices. Place each piece between two pieces of plastic wrap and roll with a rolling pin to flatten the fish. Cut each piece in half to give 32 pieces.

Thinly peel the zest from the lemons and cut the zest into 24 pieces. Squeeze the lemons to give 60 ml (2 fl oz/¹/₄ cup) juice.

Heat 2 tablespoons of the olive oil in a frying pan over medium heat. Add the chopped onion and garlic and cook for 2 minutes. Place in a bowl with the capers, olives, parmesan, breadcrumbs and parsley. Season, add the egg and mix. Divide the stuffing among the fish pieces and roll up the fish to form neat parcels. Thread four rolls onto each of eight skewers, alternating with the bay leaves, lemon zest and onion quarters.

Mix the remaining oil with the lemon juice. Barbecue the skewers for 3–4 minutes each side, basting with the oil and lemon mixture.

PREPARATION TIME: 35 MINUTES   COOKING TIME: 10 MINUTES

MUSSELS IN TOMATO AND HERB SAUCE

TOMATO AND HERB SAUCE
80 ml (2½ fl oz/⅓ cup) olive oil
3 garlic cloves, finely chopped
¼ teaspoon chilli flakes
800 g (1 lb 12 oz) tinned crushed tomatoes
pinch caster (superfine) sugar

8 slices crusty Italian bread
80 ml (2½ fl oz/⅓ cup) olive oil
2 large garlic cloves, halved
1 kg (2 lb 4 oz) black mussels
1 red onion, finely chopped
6 flat-leaf (Italian) parsley sprigs, plus extra, to garnish
2 thyme sprigs, plus extra, to garnish
2 oregano sprigs, plus extra, to garnish
250 ml (9 fl oz/1 cup) white wine

SERVES 4

Preheat the oven to 160°C (315°F/Gas 2–3). To make the tomato and herb sauce, heat the oil in a saucepan, add the garlic and chilli flakes, and cook over low heat for 30 seconds without browning. Add the tomato, sugar and 80 ml (2½ fl oz/⅓ cup) water. Season well and simmer, stirring often, for 15 minutes, or until the sauce has thickened and reduced.

Lightly brush the bread with olive oil using half the oil. Place the bread in a single layer on a baking tray and bake for 10 minutes, or until crisp and golden. While still warm, rub one side of each slice with garlic.

Meanwhile, scrub the mussels with a stiff brush and pull out the hairy beards. Discard any broken mussels, or open ones that don't close when tapped on the bench. Rinse well.

Heat the remaining olive oil in a large saucepan, add the onion and cook for 3 minutes, or until softened but not browned. Add the parsley, thyme, oregano sprigs and wine to the saucepan. Bring to the boil, then reduce the heat and simmer for 5 minutes.

Add the mussels to the pan, stir to coat in the onion and wine mixture, and cook, covered, over high heat for 3–4 minutes. Gently shake the pan often, to move the mussels around. Remove the mussels as they open. Discard any unopened mussels.

Strain the wine mixture into the tomato sauce, discarding the onion and herbs. Check the sauce for seasoning and adjust if necessary. Add the mussels and toss well to coat in the mixture. Pile into a serving bowl and garnish with the extra parsley, thyme and oregano. Arrange the toast around the bowl and serve.

PREPARATION TIME: 30 MINUTES   COOKING TIME: 40 MINUTES

NOTES: You can keep mussels (uncleaned) for a day or two longer in a bucket of cold, salted water.

Clams can be prepared in the same way as the mussels and used as a substitute in this recipe.

PARMESAN AND ROSEMARY CRUSTED VEAL CHOPS

4 veal chops
150 g (5^1/$_2$ oz) fresh white breadcrumbs
75 g (2^1/$_2$ oz/^{3}/$_4$ cup) freshly grated parmesan cheese
1 tablespoon rosemary, finely chopped
2 eggs, lightly beaten, seasoned
60 ml (2 fl oz/^{1}/$_4$ cup) olive oil
60 g (2^1/$_4$ oz) butter
4 garlic cloves

SERVES 4

Trim the chops of excess fat and sinew and flatten to 1 cm (^{1}/$_2$ inch) thickness. Pat the meat dry with paper towels. Combine the breadcrumbs, parmesan and rosemary in a shallow bowl.

Dip each chop in the beaten egg, draining off the excess. Press both sides of the chops firmly in the crumbs.

Heat the oil and butter in a heavy-based frying pan over low heat, add the garlic and cook until golden. Discard the garlic.

Increase the heat to medium, add the chops to the pan and cook for 4-5 minutes on each side, depending on the thickness of the chops, until golden and crisp. Transfer to a warm serving dish and season.

PREPARATION TIME: 15 MINUTES   COOKING TIME: 15 MINUTES

TROUT WITH ALMONDS

2 rainbow trout, or baby salmon
plain (all-purpose) flour, for coating
60 g (2^1/$_4$ oz) butter
25 g (1 oz/^{1}/$_4$ cup) flaked almonds
2 tablespoons lemon juice
1 tablespoon finely chopped flat-leaf (Italian) parsley
lemon or lime wedges, to serve

SERVES 2

Wash the fish and pat dry with paper towels. Open the fish out, skin side up. Run a rolling pin along the backbone, starting at the tail, pressing gently down. Turn the fish over and use scissors to cut through the backbone at each end of the fish. Lift out the backbone. Remove any remaining bones. Trim the fins with scissors.

Coat the fish with flour. In a large frying pan, heat half the butter and add the fish. Cook for 4 minutes each side, or until golden brown. Remove the fish and place on heated serving plates. Cover with foil.

Heat the remaining butter, add the flaked almonds and stir until light golden. Add the lemon juice, parsley, and salt and freshly ground pepper. Stir until the sauce is heated through. Pour over the fish and serve with lemon or lime wedges.

PREPARATION TIME: 25 MINUTES   COOKING TIME: 10 MINUTES

CIOPPINO

2 dried Chinese mushrooms
1 kg (2 lb 4 oz) skinless firm white fish fillets, such as hake, snapper, ocean perch or red mullet
375 g (13 oz) raw large prawns (shrimp)
1 raw lobster tail (about 400 g/14 oz)
12–15 black mussels
60 ml (2 fl oz/¼ cup) olive oil
1 large onion, finely chopped
1 green capsicum (pepper), seeded and membrane removed, finely chopped
2–3 garlic cloves, crushed
425 g (15 oz) tinned crushed tomatoes
250 ml (9 fl oz/1 cup) dry white wine
250 ml (9 fl oz/1 cup) tomato juice
250 ml (9 fl oz/1 cup) fish stock
1 bay leaf
2 flat-leaf (Italian) parsley sprigs
2 teaspoons chopped basil
1 tablespoon chopped flat-leaf (Italian) parsley, extra, to garnish

SERVES 4

Place the mushrooms in a small bowl, cover with boiling water and soak for 20 minutes. Cut the fish into bite-size pieces, removing any bones.

Peel the prawns, leaving the tails intact. Gently pull out the dark vein from each prawn back, starting at the head end.

Starting at the end where the head was, cut down the sides of the lobster shell on the underside of the lobster with kitchen scissors. Pull back the flap, remove the meat from the shell and cut into small pieces.

Scrub the mussels with a stiff brush and pull out the hairy beards. Discard any broken mussels, or open ones that don't close when tapped on the bench. Rinse well.

Drain the mushrooms, squeeze dry and chop finely. Heat the oil in a heavy-based saucepan, add the onion, capsicum and garlic and stir over medium heat for about 5 minutes, or until the onion is soft. Add the mushrooms, tomato, wine, tomato juice, stock, bay leaf, parsley sprigs and basil. Bring to the boil, reduce the heat, then cover and simmer for 30 minutes.

Layer the fish and prawns in a large frying pan. Add the sauce, then cover and leave on low heat for 10 minutes, or until the prawns are pink and the fish is cooked. Add the lobster and mussels and simmer for a further 4–5 minutes. Season. Discard any unopened mussels. Sprinkle with parsley.

PREPARATION TIME: 30 MINUTES +   COOKING TIME: 1 HOUR

FISH BAKED IN SALT

1.8 kg (4 lb) whole fish, such as
blue-eye, jewfish, sea bass, or groper,
scaled and cleaned
2 lemons, sliced
4 thyme sprigs, plus extra, to garnish
1 fennel bulb, thinly sliced
3 kg (6 lb 12 oz) rock salt
100 g (3½ oz) plain (all-purpose) flour

SERVES 6

Preheat the oven to 200°C (400°F/Gas 6). Rinse the fish and pat dry inside and out with paper towel. Place the lemon, thyme and fennel inside the cavity.

Pack half the salt into a large baking dish and place the fish on top. Cover with the remaining salt, pressing down until the salt is packed firmly around the fish.

Combine the flour with enough water to form a smooth paste, then brush, spreading carefully and evenly, over the surface of the salt. Be careful not to disturb the salt.

Bake the fish for 30–40 minutes, or until a skewer inserted into the centre of the fish comes out hot. Carefully crack open the salt crust with the back of a spoon and gently remove the skin from the fish, ensuring that no salt remains on the flesh. Garnish with thyme.

PREPARATION TIME: 20 MINUTES   COOKING TIME: 40 MINUTES

STUFFED FISH

1 kg (2 lb 4 oz) whole fish, such as
snapper, murray cod, or sea bass,
scaled and cleaned
60 ml (2 fl oz/¼ cup) lemon juice
30 g (1 oz) butter, chopped

STUFFING
2 tablespoons olive oil
1 small onion, finely chopped
3 tablespoons chopped celery leaves
2 tablespoons chopped flat-leaf (Italian)
parsley
80 g (2¾ oz/1 cup) fresh breadcrumbs
1½ tablespoons lemon juice
1 egg, lightly beaten

SERVES 4

Preheat the oven to 180°C (350°F/Gas 4). Pat the fish dry and sprinkle with salt and the lemon juice. Set aside.

To make the stuffing, heat the oil in a saucepan, add the onion and cook over medium heat for 2 minutes, or until softened. Add the celery leaves and parsley and cook, stirring, for a further 2 minutes. Spoon into a bowl, add the breadcrumbs, lemon juice and salt, to taste, then mix well. Cool slightly, then stir in the egg.

Place the stuffing in the fish cavity and secure the opening with skewers. Place the fish in a large greased baking dish and dot with butter. Bake for 30–35 minutes, or until the fish is cooked and flakes easily when tested with a fork. The thickness of the fish will determine the cooking time. Transfer to a serving dish.

PREPARATION TIME: 40 MINUTES   COOKING TIME: 45 MINUTES

Fish baked in salt

CHICKEN, VEAL AND MUSHROOM LOAF

100 g (3½ oz) pappardelle
20 g (¾ oz/¼ cup) fresh breadcrumbs
1 tablespoon dry white wine
375 g (13 oz) minced (ground) chicken
375 g (13 oz) minced (ground) veal
2 garlic cloves, crushed
100 g (3½ oz) button mushrooms, finely chopped
2 eggs, beaten
pinch freshly grated nutmeg
pinch cayenne pepper
60 g (2¼ oz/¼ cup) sour cream
4 spring onions (scallions), finely chopped
2 tablespoons chopped flat-leaf (Italian) parsley

SERVES 6

Grease a 1.5 litre (52 fl oz/6-cup) loaf tin. Cook the pappardelle in a large saucepan of rapidly boiling salted water until *al dente*. Drain.

Preheat the oven to 200°C (400°F/Gas 6). Soak the breadcrumbs in the wine. Mix the crumbs in a bowl with the chicken and veal, garlic, mushrooms, eggs, nutmeg, cayenne pepper, then season to taste. Mix in the sour cream, spring onion and parsley.

Place half the mince mixture into the prepared tin with your hands. Form a deep trough along the entire length. Fill the trough with the pappardelle. Press the remaining mince mixture over the top. Bake for 50–60 minutes, draining the excess fat and juice from the tin twice during cooking. Cool slightly before slicing.

PREPARATION TIME: 20 MINUTES   COOKING TIME: 1 HOUR

NOTE: Mushrooms can be chopped in a food processor. Don't prepare too far in advance or they will discolour and darken the loaf.

CAPONATA WITH TUNA

CAPONATA

500 g (1 lb 2 oz) ripe tomatoes
750 g (1 lb 10 oz) eggplant (aubergine),
cut into 1 cm (1/2 inch) cubes
125 ml (4 fl oz/1/2 cup) olive oil
1 onion, chopped
3 celery stalks, chopped
2 tablespoons capers, rinsed and
squeezed dry
125 g (4 1/2 oz/2/3 cup) green olives, pitted
1 tablespoon sugar
125 ml (4 fl oz/1/2 cup) red wine vinegar

6 x 200 g (7 oz) tuna steaks
olive oil, for brushing

SERVES 6

Score a cross in the base of each tomato. Place in a heatproof bowl and cover with boiling water. Leave for 30 seconds, then transfer to cold water and peel the skin away from the cross. Cut the tomatoes into 1 cm (1/2 inch) cubes.

Sprinkle the eggplant with salt and leave in a colander for 1 hour. Rinse under cold water and pat dry. Heat 2 tablespoons of the oil in a frying pan over medium heat and cook half the eggplant for 4-5 minutes, or until golden and soft. Remove from the pan and drain on crumpled paper towels. Repeat with another 2 tablespoons oil and the remaining eggplant.

Heat the remaining olive oil in the same pan, add the onion and celery, and cook for 5-6 minutes, or until softened. Reduce the heat to low, add the tomato and simmer for 15 minutes. Stir in the capers, olives, sugar and vinegar, season and continue to simmer for 10 minutes, or until slightly reduced. Stir in the eggplant. Remove from the heat and cool.

Heat a chargrill plate and brush lightly with olive oil. Cook the tuna for 2-3 minutes each side, or to your liking. Serve with the caponata.

PREPARATION TIME: 25 MINUTES +   COOKING TIME: 45 MINUTES

PAN-FRIED SALMON WITH GREMOLATA

GREMOLATA
4 tablespoons finely chopped flat-leaf
(Italian) parsley
2 teaspoons grated lemon zest
2 teaspoons grated orange zest
2 garlic cloves, crushed
3 teaspoons capers, rinsed and
squeezed dry

30 g (1 oz) butter
1 tablespoon olive oil
4 x 200 g (7 oz) salmon fillets

SERVES 4

Combine the parsley, lemon and orange zest and garlic in a small bowl with the capers. Mix well and set aside.

Heat a large frying pan and add the butter and olive oil. Add the salmon fillets and pan-fry over high heat on both sides for about 2-3 minutes each side, or until cooked as desired. Serve the salmon topped with the gremolata mixture.

PREPARATION TIME: 10 MINUTES   COOKING TIME: 10 MINUTES

Caponata with tuna

OSSO BUCCO ALLA MILANESE

12 pieces veal shank, about 4 cm
(1^1/$_2$ inch) thick
plain (all-purpose) flour, seasoned,
for dusting
60 ml (2 fl oz/^{1}/$_4$ cup) olive oil
60 g (2^1/$_4$ oz) butter
1 garlic clove, finely chopped
1 onion, finely chopped
1 celery stalk, finely chopped
250 ml (9 fl oz/1 cup) dry white wine
1 bay leaf or lemon leaf
pinch ground allspice
pinch ground cinnamon

GREMOLATA
2 teaspoons grated lemon zest
2 tablespoons finely chopped flat-leaf
(Italian) parsley
1 garlic clove, finely chopped

SERVES 4

Dust each piece of veal shank with seasoned flour. Heat the oil, butter, garlic, onion and celery in a heavy-based frying pan or saucepan that is big enough to hold the shanks in a single layer (but don't add the shanks yet). Cook for about 5 minutes over low heat until softened but not browned. Add the shanks to the pan and cook for 12–15 minutes, or until well browned all over. Arrange the shanks in the pan, standing them up in a single layer. Pour in the wine and add the bay leaf, allspice and cinnamon. Bring to the boil and cover the pan. Turn the heat down to low.

Cook at a low simmer for 15 minutes, then add 125 ml (4 fl oz/^{1}/$_2$ cup) warm water. Continue cooking, covered, for 45–60 minutes (the timing will depend on the age of the veal) or until the meat is tender and you can cut it with a fork. Check the volume of liquid once or twice during cooking time and add more warm water as needed.

To make the gremolata, mix together the lemon zest, parsley and garlic.

Transfer the veal shanks to a plate and keep warm. Discard the bay leaf. Increase the heat under the pan and stir for 1–2 minutes until the sauce has thickened, scraping up any bits off the bottom of the pan as you stir. Season to taste and return the veal shanks to the sauce. Heat everything through, then stir in half the gremolata. Serve sprinkled with the remaining gremolata.

PREPARATION TIME: 30 MINUTES   COOKING TIME: 1 HOUR 40 MINUTES

SALADS AND VEGETABLES

TOMATO AND BOCCONCINI SALAD

3 large vine-ripened tomatoes
250 g (9 oz) bocconcini (fresh baby mozarella cheese)
12 basil leaves
60 ml (2 fl oz/¼ cup) extra virgin olive oil

SERVES 4

Slice the tomato into twelve 1 cm (¹/₂ inch) slices. Slice the bocconcini into 24 slices the same thickness as the tomato.

Arrange the tomato slices on a plate, alternating them with two slices of bocconcini and placing a basil leaf between the bocconcini slices.

Drizzle with the olive oil and season well.

PREPARATION TIME: 10 MINUTES   COOKING TIME: NIL

NOTE: You could use whole cherry tomatoes and toss them with the bocconcini and basil.

GARLIC CREAM MUSHROOMS

30 g (1 oz) butter
250 g (9 oz) button mushrooms, sliced
2 garlic cloves, crushed
250 ml (9 fl oz/1 cup) pouring (whipping) cream
1 tablespoon chopped flat-leaf (Italian) parsley

SERVES 4

Heat the butter in a saucepan. Add the sliced mushrooms and crushed garlic. Stir over medium heat for 3–5 minutes until the mushrooms are soft.

Turn the heat to high, add the cream and bring to the boil. Reduce to a simmer for 3 minutes until the cream has thickened slightly. Add the chopped parsley and then season to taste.

PREPARATION TIME: 10 MINUTES   COOKING TIME: 10 MINUTES

SHAVED FENNEL SALAD

2 round fennel bulbs
extra virgin olive oil

SERVES 4

Trim two round fennel bulbs by cutting off the tops where they meet the bulb. Reserve any of the small green fronds and discard the tops. Remove any tough outer parts of the bulb that are bruised or discoloured. Slice off 3 mm ($1/8$ inch) from the end and slice the bulb horizontally into paper-thin rings.

Soak the slices in two changes of cold water for 5 minutes, then drain well and pat dry with a paper towel or clean tea towel (dish towel). Toss in a serving bowl with enough extra virgin olive oil to coat well. Season.

PREPARATION TIME: 10 MINUTES   COOKING TIME: NIL

BAKED EGGPLANT WITH TOMATO AND MOZZARELLA

6 large slender eggplants (aubergines), halved lengthways, leaving the stems attached
100 ml (3½ fl oz) olive oil
2 onions, finely chopped
2 garlic cloves, crushed
400 g (14 oz) tinned chopped tomatoes
1 tablespoon tomato paste (concentrated purée)
3 tablespoons chopped flat-leaf (Italian) parsley
1 tablespoon chopped oregano
125 g (4½ oz) mozzarella cheese, grated

SERVES 6

Preheat the oven to 180°C (350°F/Gas 4). Score the eggplant flesh by cutting a criss-cross pattern with a sharp knife, being careful not to cut through the skin. Heat 2 tablespoons of the oil in a large frying pan, add three eggplants and cook for 2–3 minutes each side, or until the flesh is soft. Remove. Repeat with another 2 tablespoons of the oil and the remaining eggplants. Cool slightly and scoop out the flesh, leaving a 2 mm (1/16 inch) border. Finely chop the flesh and reserve the shells.

In the same pan, heat the remaining oil and cook the onion over medium heat for 5 minutes. Add the garlic and cook for 30 seconds, then add the tomato, tomato paste, herbs and eggplant flesh, and cook, stirring occasionally, over low heat for 8–10 minutes, or until the sauce is thick and pulpy. Season well.

Arrange the eggplant shells in a lightly greased baking dish and spoon in the tomato filling. Sprinkle with mozzarella and bake for 5–10 minutes, or until the cheese has melted.

PREPARATION TIME: 20 MINUTES   COOKING TIME: 40 MINUTES

ROCKET AND PECORINO SALAD

60 ml (2 fl oz/¼ cup) extra virgin olive oil
2 tablespoons lemon juice
150 g (5½ oz) rocket (arugula) leaves
pecorino cheese, to serve

SERVES 4

Combine the oil with the lemon juice and salt and pepper in a bowl. Add the rocket leaves and toss lightly to coat. Place in a serving dish.

Using a vegetable peeler, shave thin curls of pecorino over the salad. Adjust the seasoning and serve.

PREPARATION TIME: 10 MINUTES   COOKING TIME: NIL

SAUTÉED MUSHROOMS WITH GARLIC

750 g (1 lb 10 oz) mushroom caps, such as field, Swiss brown or any wild mushroom
80 ml (2½ fl oz/⅓ cup) extra virgin olive oil
2 teaspoons crushed garlic
1 teaspoon chopped thyme
3 tablespoons chopped flat-leaf (Italian) parsley

SERVES 4–6

Wipe any dirt off the mushroom caps. Trim the stems and thinly slice the mushrooms, keeping the stems and caps intact.

Heat the extra virgin olive oil in a large heavy-based frying pan and cook the garlic over low heat until it colours lightly but does not brown. Add the thyme and mushrooms and toss. Increase the heat, season and cook for 10 minutes, or until the mushrooms have soaked up all the oil and softened. Reduce the heat to low and cook, stirring with a wooden spoon, until the mushrooms release their juices. Return the heat to high and cook for 4–5 minutes, or until the juices have evaporated. Adjust the seasoning, add the parsley and combine. Serve warm or at room temperature.

PREPARATION TIME: 10 MINUTES   COOKING TIME: 20 MINUTES

Rocket and pecorino salad

PANZANELLA

1 small red onion, thinly sliced
250 g (9 oz) stale bread such as ciabatta, crusts removed
4 ripe tomatoes
6 anchovy fillets, finely chopped
1 small garlic clove, crushed
1 tablespoon baby capers, rinsed, squeezed dry and chopped
2 tablespoons red wine vinegar
125 ml (4 fl oz/$\frac{1}{2}$ cup) extra virgin olive oil
2 small Lebanese (short) cucumbers, peeled and sliced
30 g (1 oz) basil leaves, torn

SERVES 6–8

In a small bowl, cover the onion with cold water and leave for 5 minutes. Squeeze the rings in your hand, closing tightly and letting go and repeating that process about five times. This removes the acid from the onion. Repeat the whole process twice more, using fresh water each time.

Tear the bread into rough 3 cm (1$\frac{1}{4}$ inch) squares and toast lightly under a grill (broiler) for 4 minutes, or until bread is crisp but not browned. Allow to cool. Set aside.

Score a cross in the base of each tomato. Put in a heatproof bowl and cover with boiling water. Leave for 30 seconds, then transfer to cold water, drain and peel away the skin from the cross. Cut each tomato in half and scoop out the seeds. Roughly chop two of the tomatoes and purée the other two.

Combine the anchovies, garlic and capers in a bowl. Add the vinegar and olive oil and whisk to combine. Season, then transfer to a large bowl and add the bread, onion, puréed and chopped tomato, cucumber and basil. Toss well and season, to taste. Leave to stand for at least 15 minutes to allow the flavours to develop. Serve at room temperature.

PREPARATION TIME: 30 MINUTES +   COOKING TIME: 5 MINUTES

GREEN BEANS WITH GARLIC BREADCRUMBS

600 g (1 lb 5 oz) trimmed baby green beans
60 ml (2 fl oz/¼ cup) olive oil
4 garlic cloves, peeled
40 g (1½ oz/½ cup) fresh breadcrumbs
2 tablespoons chopped flat-leaf (Italian) parsley

SERVES 4

Cook the baby green beans, in a large saucepan of boiling salted water until tender but still firm. Drain and refresh under cold running water. Drain again and pat dry with paper towels.

Heat the olive oil in a heavy-based frying pan and cook the garlic cloves until golden brown. Remove and discard. Add the breadcrumbs to the oil and cook over low heat, stirring constantly for 3–4 minutes, or until the crumbs are brown and crunchy. Add the beans and parsley to the pan, then season to taste. Stir to mix with the breadcrumbs and warm the beans. Can be served warm or at room temperature.

PREPARATION TIME: 10 MINUTES   COOKING TIME: 15 MINUTES

BEAN SALAD WITH VINAIGRETTE

VINAIGRETTE DRESSING
2 tablespoons walnut oil
1 tablespoon balsamic vinegar
1 garlic clove, crushed

800 g (1 lb 12 oz) tinned cannellini or haricot beans, rinsed and drained
4 spring onions (scallions), finely chopped
2 tablespoons finely chopped flat-leaf (Italian) parsley
1 small handful torn basil leaves

SERVES 4

Make the vinaigrette dressing by thoroughly whisking together the walnut oil, balsamic vinegar and crushed garlic.

Combine the beans, spring onions, parsley and basil in a large bowl. Season well. Toss through the dressing. Allow to stand for about 10 minutes before serving so the beans soak up the flavour.

PREPARATION TIME: 10 MINUTES   COOKING TIME: NIL

Green beans with garlic breadcrumbs

FENNEL FRITTERS

1 kg (2 lb 4 oz) fennel bulbs (see Note)
30 g (1 oz/¹/₃ cup) grated pecorino cheese
80 g (2³/₄ oz/1 cup) fresh breadcrumbs
60 g (2¹/₄ oz/¹/₂ cup) plain (all-purpose) flour
3 eggs, lightly beaten
olive oil, for pan-frying
lemon wedges, to serve

SERVES 4

Remove the tough outer leaves from the fennel, then trim the base and small stalks. Slice the fennel lengthways at 5 mm (¹/₄ inch) intervals and blanch in boiling salted water for 3 minutes, or until tender. Drain and pat dry. Leave to cool.

Mix together the cheese and breadcrumbs and season.

Coat the fennel in flour, shake off the excess and dip in beaten egg. Coat in the crumb and cheese mix. Heat the oil in large heavy-based frying pan until the oil beings to sizzle. Fry the fennel in batches, being careful not to overcrowd the pan, for 2–3 minutes per side, until golden brown and crisp. Drain on paper towels, season and serve immediately with the lemon wedges.

PREPARATION TIME: 15 MINUTES   COOKING TIME: 20 MINUTES

NOTE: Use the rounder, male fennel bulbs, rather than the flatter female bulbs, as they have more flavour.

BAKED RADICCHIO

1 kg (2 lb 4 oz) radicchio
2 tablespoons olive oil
100 g (3½ oz) bacon, thinly sliced

SERVES 4

Preheat the oven to 180°C (350°F/Gas 4). Remove the outer leaves of the radicchio and split the heads into four wedges.

Heat the olive oil in a flameproof casserole dish large enough to fit all the radicchio in a single layer (but do not add the radicchio yet). Add the bacon and cook over medium heat until the fat has just melted but the meat is not crisp. Add the radicchio and turn it over to coat it well. Bake, covered, for 25–30 minutes, until tender when pierced with a knife, turning the radicchio occasionally. Season and transfer to a warm dish with all the liquid. Serve immediately.

PREPARATION TIME: 10 MINUTES   COOKING TIME: 30 MINUTES

STUFFED MUSHROOMS

8 large cap mushrooms
80 ml (2½ fl oz/⅓ cup) olive oil
30 g (1 oz) prosciutto, finely chopped
1 garlic clove, crushed
2 tablespoons soft fresh breadcrumbs
30 g (1 oz) freshly grated parmesan cheese
2 tablespoons chopped flat-leaf (Italian) parsley

SERVES 4

Preheat the oven to 190°C (375°F/Gas 5). Lightly grease a baking dish. Remove the mushroom stalks and finely chop them.

Heat 1 tablespoon of the oil in a frying pan, add the prosciutto, garlic and mushroom stalks and cook for 5 minutes. Mix in a bowl with the breadcrumbs, parmesan and parsley.

Brush the mushroom caps with 1 tablespoon of the olive oil and place them, gill side up, on the baking dish. Divide the stuffing among the caps and bake for 20 minutes. Drizzle with the remaining oil and serve hot or warm.

PREPARATION TIME: 10 MINUTES   COOKING TIME: 25 MINUTES

FENNEL, TOMATO AND WHITE BEAN STEW

5 tomatoes, peeled, seeded and chopped

2 leeks, washed and sliced

2 garlic cloves, finely chopped

1 large fennel bulb, washed, halved, cored and sliced

60 ml (2 fl oz/¼ cup) extra virgin olive oil

60 ml (2 fl oz/¼ cup) Pernod

2 bay leaves

5 thyme sprigs

500 g (1 lb 2 oz) all-purpose potatoes, peeled and cut into large chunks

400 g (14 oz) tinned cannellini beans, rinsed and drained

250 ml (9 fl oz/1 cup) vegetable stock

250 ml (9 fl oz/1 cup) dry white wine

125 g (4½ oz/½ cup) ready-made pesto, to serve

SERVES 4–6

Preheat the oven to 180°C (350°F/Gas 4). In a large ovenproof dish combine the tomato, leek, garlic, fennel, oil, Pernod, bay leaves, and thyme. Mix well. (This should preferably be done well ahead of time to allow the flavours to develop.)

Cover the dish and bake for 30 minutes. Remove from the oven. Add the potato, beans, stock and wine. Mix well and cover. Bake for a further 35–45 minutes, or until the potatoes are cooked through. Remove the bay leaves and thyme and discard them. Serve in warmed bowls, with a spoonful of pesto.

PREPARATION TIME: 25 MINUTES   COOKING TIME: 1 HOUR 15 MINUTES

ROSEMARY POTATOES

125 ml (4 fl oz/½ cup) extra virgin
olive oil
two 12 cm (5 inch) rosemary sprigs
8 garlic cloves, unpeeled
1.5 kg (3 lb 5 oz) roasting potatoes, cut
into 4 cm (1½ inch) cubes
sea salt, to season

SERVES 6

Preheat the oven to 180°C (350°F/Gas 4). Pour the oil into a large baking dish, add the rosemary, garlic and potato and toss to coat.

Bake on the centre rack for 30 minutes. Turn the potatoes and sprinkle with sea salt. Bake for a further 30 minutes, or until the potatoes are crisp and golden. Serve warm.

PREPARATION TIME: 5 MINUTES   COOKING TIME: 1 HOUR

SAUTÉED SILVERBEET

1 kg (2 lb 4 oz) silverbeet (Swiss chard)
2 tablespoons olive oil
3 garlic cloves, thinly sliced
extra virgin olive oil, to serve

SERVES 4–6

Trim the leaves from the stalks of the silverbeet and rinse them in cold water. Blanch the leaves in a large saucepan of boiling, salted water for 1–2 minutes, or until tender but still firm. Drain well in a colander. Lay out on a tea towel (dish towel) or tray to cool, then, using your hands, gently wring out the excess water from the leaves.

Heat the oil in a heavy-based frying pan and cook the garlic over low heat until just starting to turn golden. Add the silverbeet, season and cook over medium heat for 3–4 minutes, or until warmed through. Transfer to a serving plate and drizzle with extra virgin olive oil. Serve warm or at room temperature.

PREPARATION TIME: 15 MINUTES   COOKING TIME: 10 MINUTES

NOTE: This is delicious eaten warm with meat or fish, or at room temperature with bruschetta, as part of an antipasto platter.

ROMAN-STYLE ARTICHOKES

4 globe artichokes
60 ml (2 fl oz/¼ cup) lemon juice
1 tablespoon fresh breadcrumbs, toasted
1 large garlic clove, crushed
3 tablespoons finely chopped flat-leaf (Italian) parsley
3 tablespoons finely chopped mint
1½ tablespoons olive oil
60 ml (2 fl oz/¼ cup) dry white wine

SERVES 4

Preheat the oven to 190°C (375°F/Gas 5). Add the lemon juice to a large bowl of cold water. Remove the tough outer leaves from the artichokes and trim the stalks to 5 cm (2 inches) long. Peel the stalks with a potato peeler. Slice off the top quarter of each artichoke with a sharp knife to give a level surface. Gently open out the leaves and scrape out the hairy choke, using a teaspoon or a small sharp knife. Drop each artichoke into the lemon water as you go.

Combine the breadcrumbs, garlic, parsley, mint and olive oil in a bowl and season well. Fill the centre of each artichoke with the mixture, pressing it in well. Close the leaves as tightly as possible to prevent the filling from falling out.

Arrange the artichokes with the stalks up in a deep casserole dish just large enough to fit them so they are tightly packed. Sprinkle with salt and pour in the wine. Cover with a lid, or a double sheet of kitchen foil secured tightly at the edges. Bake for about 1½ hours, until very tender. Serve hot as a first course or side vegetable, or at room temperature as an antipasto.

PREPARATION TIME: 25 MINUTES   COOKING TIME: 1 HOUR 30 MINUTES

NOTE: Check the artichokes halfway through cooking and, if necessary, add a little water to prevent them from burning.

BRAISED LEEKS WITH PINE NUTS

20 g (³/4 oz) butter
2 teaspoons olive oil
2 leeks, trimmed and thinly sliced
80 ml (2¹/2 fl oz/¹/3 cup) vegetable stock
80 ml (2¹/2 fl oz/¹/3 cup) dry white wine
2 tablespoons finely chopped mixed
herbs, such as flat-leaf (Italian)
parsley and oregano
1 tablespoon pine nuts, lightly toasted
1 tablespoon freshly grated parmesan
cheese

SERVES 4

Heat the butter and oil in a large frying pan. Cook the leeks, stirring, for 5 minutes, or until golden brown.

Add the vegetable stock and white wine. Cook for a further 10 minutes, or until the leeks are tender. Stir through the fresh herbs. Sprinkle with toasted pine nuts and the parmesan. Serve immediately.

PREPARATION TIME: 10 MINUTES   COOKING TIME: 15 MINUTES

CHERRY TOMATOES WITH BUTTER AND DILL

30 g (1 oz) butter
400 g (14 oz) cherry tomatoes
1 tablespoon finely chopped dill

SERVES 4

Heat the butter in a frying pan. Toss the tomatoes until the skins are beginning to split. Season well and sprinkle with the chopped dill. Gently toss and serve immediately.

PREPARATION TIME: 5 MINUTES   COOKING TIME: 5 MINUTES

Braised leeks with pine nuts

FENNEL, ORANGE AND ALMOND SALAD

2 fennel bulbs, trimmed

3 oranges

100 g (3^1/$_2$ oz) flaked almonds

150 g (5^1/$_2$ oz) creamy blue cheese, crumbled

50 g (1^3/$_4$ oz) sun-dried (sun-blushed) capsicum (pepper), thinly sliced (see Note)

DRESSING

80 ml (2^1/$_2$ fl oz/^{1}/$_3$ cup) orange juice

1 tablespoon red wine vinegar

1 teaspoon sesame oil

SERVES 4

Thinly slice the fennel bulbs. Peel the oranges, removing all the white pith, and cut into segments. Toast the flaked almonds in a dry frying pan until golden.

Combine the fennel, orange and almonds in a bowl. Add the crumbled blue cheese and the sun-dried capsicum. Gently toss to combine.

Make the dressing by combining the orange juice, red wine vinegar and sesame oil. Drizzle over the salad and serve.

PREPARATION TIME: 10 MINUTES   COOKING TIME: 5 MINUTES

NOTE: Pat the sun-dried capsicum with paper towels to remove excess oil.

HERB SALAD

100 g (3½ oz) baby rocket
(arugula) leaves
100 g (3½ oz) baby English spinach
leaves
1 small handful basil leaves
15 g (½ oz) chopped flat-leaf (Italian)
parsley
15 g (½ oz) chopped coriander (cilantro)
leaves

DRESSING
2 tablespoons olive oil
1 tablespoon lemon juice
1 garlic clove, crushed
1 teaspoon honey

SERVES 4

Combine the rocket and spinach leaves with the basil, parsley and coriander in a bowl.

To make the dressing, combine the oil and lemon with the garlic and honey. Drizzle over the dressing. Toss well and serve immediately with freshly cracked black pepper.

PREPARATION TIME: 10 MINUTES   COOKING TIME: NIL

ROAST PUMPKIN WITH SAGE

1 kg (2 lb 4 oz) pumpkin (winter squash),
peeled and seeded
olive oil, to coat
2 tablespoon chopped sage, plus extra,
to garnish

SERVES 4

Preheat the oven to 220°C (425°C/Gas 7). Cut the pumpkin into small cubes and toss well in olive oil. Transfer to a baking dish and scatter with the sage and season well.

Bake for 20 minutes, or until lightly browned. Serve scattered with extra sage.

PREPARATION TIME: 10 MINUTES   COOKING TIME: 20 MINUTES

MIXED TOMATO SALAD

200 g (7 oz) cherry tomatoes
200 g (7 oz) teardrop tomatoes
2 small roma (plum) tomatoes, sliced
1 small red onion, finely chopped
1 small handful basil, finely
shredded
2 tablespoons olive oil
1 tablespoon red wine vinegar

SERVES 4

Toss the cherry, teardrop and roma tomatoes in a bowl with the onion and basil leaves.

Combine the olive oil and red wine vinegar. Drizzle over the dressing, gently toss through the salad and serve immediately.

PREPARATION TIME: 5 MINUTES   COOKING TIME: NIL

NOTES: Tomatoes should be stored at cool room temperature, not in the refrigerator as this diminishes the flavour. Use tomatoes within a few days.

If you purchase under-ripe tomatoes they will ripen fully, given the right conditions. Place them somewhere warm and in full sunlight.

ZUCCHINI WITH LEMON AND CAPER BUTTER

LEMON AND CAPER BUTTER
100 g (3¹/2 oz) butter, softened
2 tablespoons capers, rinsed, squeezed
dry and chopped
2 teaspoons grated lemon zest
1 tablespoon lemon juice

8 small zucchini (courgettes)

SERVES 4

To make the lemon and caper butter, combine the butter with the capers, lemon zest and juice in a small bowl. Season well.

Thinly slice the zucchini lengthways and steam in a saucepan for 3–5 minutes, or until tender. Toss with the lemon and caper butter and serve immediately.

PREPARATION TIME: 5 MINUTES   COOKING TIME: 5 MINUTES

BROAD BEANS WITH PEAS AND ARTICHOKES

2 onions
2 tablespoons dill
1 tablespoon mint leaves
60 ml (2 fl oz/¹/4 cup) olive oil
250 g (9 oz) frozen broad (fava) beans
2 tablespoons lemon juice
250 g (9 oz) frozen peas
400 g (14 oz) tinned artichoke hearts,
drained, halved
4 spring onions (scallions), chopped

SERVES 4–6

Slice the onions into rings. Finely chop the dill and mint.

Heat the oil in a large saucepan. Add the onion. Stir over low heat for 5 minutes, or until soft and golden.

Add the beans, lemon juice and 125 ml (4 fl oz/¹/2 cup) water to the pan. Bring to the boil, reduce the heat and simmer, covered, for 5 minutes.

Add the peas, artichoke hearts and herbs. Simmer, covered, for 5 minutes, or until the peas are just tender, but not soft. Remove from the heat, stir in the spring onions, then season. Serve warm or at room temperature.

PREPARATION TIME: 15 MINUTES   COOKING TIME: 15 MINUTES

Zucchini with lemon and caper butter

MARINATED BARBECUED VEGETABLES

3 small slender eggplants (aubergines)
2 small red capsicums (peppers)
3 zucchini (courgettes)
6 mushrooms

MARINADE
60 ml (2 fl oz/¼ cup) olive oil
60 ml (2 fl oz/¼ cup) lemon juice
2 tablespoons shredded basil
1 garlic clove, crushed

SERVES 4–6

Cut the eggplants into diagonal slices. Place on a baking tray in a single layer, sprinkle with salt and allow to stand for 15 minutes. Rinse thoroughly and pat dry with paper towels. Trim the capsicums, remove the seeds and membrane and cut into long, wide pieces. Cut the zucchinis into diagonal slices. Trim each mushroom stalk so that it is level with the cap. Place all the vegetables in a large, shallow non-metal dish.

To make the marinade, combine the oil, lemon juice, basil and garlic in a bowl. Whisk until well combined. Pour the marinade over the vegetables and stir gently. Store, covered with plastic wrap, in the refrigerator for 1 hour, stirring occasionally. Prepare and heat a barbecue grill or flat plate.

Place the vegetables on the hot, lightly greased barbecue grill. Cook pieces over the hottest part of the fire for 2 minutes on each side. Transfer to a serving dish once browned. Brush the vegetables frequently with any remaining marinade while cooking.

PREPARATION TIME: 40 MINUTES +   COOKING TIME: 5 MINUTES

NOTE: Vegetables can be marinated for up to 2 hours. Take them out of the refrigerator 15 minutes before cooking. This dish can be served warm or at room temperature. Serve any leftovers with thick slices of crusty bread or individual bread rolls. Other herbs, such as parsley, rosemary or thyme, can be added to the marinade. The marinade also makes a great salad dressing.

TOMATO, EGG AND OLIVE SALAD

6 ripe tomatoes
1 red onion, thinly sliced
6 hard-boiled eggs, peeled and sliced
90 g (3¼ oz/½ cup) marinated
black olives
a few torn basil leaves, to serve
extra virgin olive oil, to drizzle

SERVES 4

Cut the tomatoes into thick slices and arrange on a large plate. Top with the onion, eggs and olives and scatter the basil leaves over the top.

Drizzle with some extra virgin olive oil and sprinkle generously with sea salt and freshly cracked black pepper.

PREPARATION TIME: 15 MINUTES   COOKING TIME: NIL

GREEN BEANS IN TOMATO SAUCE

300 g (10½ oz) green beans, trimmed
1 tablespoon olive oil
1 onion, finely chopped
2 garlic cloves, finely chopped
1 tablespoon paprika
¼ teaspoon chilli flakes
1 bay leaf, crushed
400 g (14 oz) tinned crushed tomatoes
2 tablespoons chopped flat-leaf
(Italian) parsley

SERVES 4

Cook the beans in boiling water for 3–5 minutes or until tender. Drain and set aside.

Heat the oil in a frying pan. Add the onion and cook over medium heat for 5 minutes, or until soft. Add the garlic and cook for 1 minute. Add the paprika, chilli flakes and bay leaf, cook for 1 minute, then add the tomato. Simmer over medium heat for 15 minutes, or until reduced and pulpy. Add the beans and parsley and cook for 1 minute, or until warmed through. Season, to taste. Serve warm or at room temperature.

PREPARATION TIME: 10 MINUTES   COOKING TIME: 30 MINUTES

Tomato, egg and olive salad

EGGPLANT WITH TOMATO HERB SAUCE

6–8 slender eggplants (aubergines)
olive oil, for pan-frying, plus
2 tablespoons, extra
2 garlic cloves, crushed
1 onion, chopped
1 red capsicum (pepper), seeded and
membrane removed, chopped
2 ripe tomatoes, chopped
125 ml (4 fl oz/½ cup) vegetable stock
1 teaspoon finely chopped thyme
1 teaspoon finely chopped marjoram
2 teaspoons finely chopped oregano
1 teaspoon sugar
3–4 teaspoons white wine vinegar
3 tablespoons small black olives
1 handful basil leaves, shredded

Cut the eggplants in half lengthways. Pour enough oil into a large frying pan to cover the base. Heat until the oil is almost smoking. Fry the eggplant in batches over medium–high heat for 2–3 minutes on each side, or until golden brown. Remove from the pan with tongs and drain on paper towels. Add more oil, if necessary, to cook each batch. Cover the eggplants and keep warm.

Heat the extra oil in a frying pan and add the garlic and onion. Stir over medium heat for 2–3 minutes. Add the capsicum and tomato. Cook, stirring, for 1–2 minutes, or until just softened.

Add the stock to the pan. Bring to the boil. Reduce the heat and simmer, stirring occasionally, for 5–10 minutes or until the liquid reduces and thickens. Stir in the thyme, marjoram, oregano, sugar and vinegar. Cook for a further 3–4 minutes. Stir in the olives. Season. Serve the warm eggplant topped with the tomato sauce and the shredded basil.

SERVES 4   PREPARATION TIME: 30 MINUTES   COOKING TIME: 40 MINUTES

NOTE: The tomato mixture can be made a day ahead, without the herbs. Add herbs when reheating — this helps to retain the colour and will ensure the flavour does not become bitter.

DESSERTS

SICILIAN CHEESECAKE

250 g (9 oz/2 cups) plain (all-purpose) flour
165 g (5³/4 oz) unsalted butter, chopped
55 g (2¹/4 oz/¹/4 cup) caster (superfine) sugar
1 teaspoon grated lemon zest
1 egg, lightly beaten

FILLING
60 g (2¹/4 oz) raisins, chopped
80 ml (2¹/2 fl oz/¹/3 cup) Marsala
500 g (1 lb 2 oz) ricotta cheese
115 g (4 oz/¹/2 cup) caster (superfine) sugar
1 tablespoon plain (all-purpose) flour
4 eggs, separated
125 ml (4 fl oz/¹/2 cup) pouring (whipping) cream

SERVES 8

Lightly grease a 26 cm (10¹/2 inch) diameter spring-form cake tin. Sift the flour and a pinch of salt into a large bowl and rub in the butter, using just your fingertips. Add the sugar, lemon zest, egg and a little water, if necessary and, using a knife, cut through until a rough dough forms. Gather the dough together into a ball.

Roll out the dough between two sheets of baking paper to fit the base and side of the tin, then chill for 30 minutes. Preheat the oven to 190°C (375°F/Gas 5). Prick the pastry base, line with baking paper and fill with dried beans or rice. Bake for 15 minutes, remove the beans and paper and bake for 8 minutes, or until the pastry is dry. If the base puffs up, gently press down with the back of a spoon. Allow to cool. Reduce the oven temperature to 160°C (315°F/Gas 2–3).

To make the filling, put the raisins and Marsala in a small bowl, cover and leave to soak. Push the ricotta through a sieve, then beat with the sugar, using a wooden spoon, until combined. Add the flour and egg yolks, then the cream and undrained raisins and mix well. In a clean, dry bowl, beat the egg whites until soft peaks form, then fold into the ricotta mixture in two batches.

Pour the filling into the pastry case and bake for 1 hour, or until just set. Check during cooking and cover with foil if the pastry is overbrowning. Cool a little in the oven with the door ajar to prevent sinking. Serve warm.

PREPARATION TIME: 45 MINUTES +   COOKING TIME: 1 HOUR 25 MINUTES

NOTE: Marsala is a fortified dark wine made in Sicily with a deep rich flavour. It is available in dry and sweet varieties. Sweet Marsala is used in desserts and as a dessert wine.

STRAWBERRIES WITH BALSAMIC VINEGAR

750 g (1 lb 10 oz) ripe small strawberries

55 g (2^1/$_4$ oz/^{1}/$_4$ cup) caster (superfine) sugar

2 tablespoons balsamic vinegar

125 g (4^1/$_2$ oz/^{1}/$_2$ cup) mascarpone cheese, to serve

SERVES 4

Wipe the strawberries with a clean damp cloth and hull them. If using large strawberries, cut them in half.

Place the strawberries in a glass bowl, sprinkle the sugar evenly over the top and toss gently to coat. Leave for 30 minutes to macerate. Sprinkle the vinegar over the strawberries, toss and refrigerate for 30 minutes.

Spoon the strawberries into four glasses, drizzle with the syrup and top with a dollop of mascarpone.

PREPARATION TIME: 10 MINUTES + COOKING TIME: NIL

ZABAGLIONE

4 egg yolks

80 g (2^3/$_4$ oz/^{1}/$_3$ cup) caster (superfine) sugar

80 ml (2^1/$_2$ fl oz/^{1}/$_3$ cup) Marsala

SERVES 4

Combine all the ingredients in a large heatproof bowl set over a saucepan of barely simmering water. Make sure the base of the bowl does not touch the water. Whisk with a balloon whisk or electric beaters for 5 minutes, or until the mixture is smooth and foamy and has tripled in volume. Do not stop whisking and do not allow the bowl to become too hot or the eggs will scramble. The final result will be creamy, pale and mousse-like.

Pour the zabaglione into four glasses and serve immediately.

PREPARATION TIME: 5 MINUTES   COOKING TIME: 10 MINUTES

NOTE: Sometimes zabaglione is served chilled. If you want to do this, cover the glasses with plastic wrap and refrigerate for at least 1 hour. You must make sure the zabaglione is properly cooked or it may separate when left to stand.

RICE ICE CREAM

110 g (3³/₄ oz/¹/₂ cup) risotto rice
750 ml (26 fl oz/3 cups) milk
1 vanilla bean
55 g (2¹/₄ oz/¹/₄ cup) sugar
500 ml (17 fl oz/2 cups) thick
(double/heavy) cream
3 teaspoons icing (confectioners') sugar
2 tablespoons finely chopped candied
citron

CUSTARD
125 ml (4 fl oz/¹/₂ cup) milk
3 egg yolks
110 g (3³/₄ oz/¹/₂ cup) sugar

SERVES 4

Put the rice in a saucepan, add the milk, vanilla bean, sugar and a pinch of salt. Bring to a boil over medium heat, stirring constantly. Reduce the heat to low and simmer for about 12 minutes. Remove the rice from the heat and set aside for about 2 hours to cool completely.

Pour the contents of the pan through a colander and drain away the excess liquid. Allow the rice stand for 30 minutes.

To make the custard, heat the milk in a saucepan over medium heat until it is almost boiling. In a bowl, whisk together the egg yolks and sugar, and add the milk. Mix well. Rinse the pan and return the milk mixture to the pan. Cook, stirring constantly, over a low heat until the custard thickens and will easily coat the back of a wooden spoon. Remove the custard from the heat and allow to cool.

Transfer the rice to a bowl, remove the vanilla bean, add the custard and mix well. Add the cream, icing sugar and candied citron, and stir well to combine.

Pour the mixture into a shallow metal tray and freeze for 1 hour. Take the tray out of the freezer and give the mixture a good stir, then refreeze. Repeat this process four times until the mixture is almost solid. The more you stir, the less icy the mixture. Alternatively, you can freeze the mixture in an ice-cream machine, following the manufacturer's instructions.

Remove the ice cream from the freezer 10 minutes before serving to soften. If it is too frozen the rice grains will be very hard.

PREPARATION TIME: 20 MINUTES +   COOKING TIME: 25 MINUTES

POACHED PEARS WITH GINGER ZABAGLIONE

500 ml (17 fl oz/2 cups) red wine
4 pieces crystallized ginger
110 g (3³/4 oz/¹/2 cup) sugar
6 pears, peeled

GINGER ZABAGLIONE
8 egg yolks
80 g (2³/4 oz/¹/3 cup) caster (superfine) sugar
1 teaspoon ground ginger
310 ml (10³/4 fl oz/1¹/4 cups) Marsala

MAKES 6

Put the wine, ginger and sugar in a large saucepan with 1 litre (35 fl oz/ 4 cups) water and stir over medium heat until the sugar has dissolved. Add the pears, cover and simmer for 45 minutes, or until tender.

To make the zabaglione, put a large saucepan half-filled with water on to boil. When boiling, remove from the heat. Beat the egg yolks, sugar and ginger in a metal or heatproof bowl, using electric beaters, until pale yellow. Set the bowl over the saucepan of steaming water, making sure the base of the bowl does not touch the water, and beat continuously, adding the Marsala gradually. Beat for 5 minutes, or until very thick and foamy and like a mousse.

Remove the pears from the pan with a slotted spoon. Arrange on plates and pour ginger zabaglione over each. Serve immediately.

PREPARATION TIME: 30 MINUTES   COOKING TIME: 1 HOUR

STUFFED PEACHES

6 ripe peaches
60 g (2¹/4 oz) amaretti biscuits, crushed
1 egg yolk
2 tablespoons caster (superfine) sugar
20 g (³/4 oz) ground almonds
1 tablespoon amaretto
60 ml (2 fl oz/¹/4 cup) sweet white wine
1 teaspoon caster (superfine) sugar, extra
20 g (³/4 oz) unsalted butter

SERVES 6

Preheat the oven to 180°C (350°F/Gas 4) and lightly grease a 25 x 30 cm (10 x 12 inch) ovenproof dish with butter.

Cut each peach in half and carefully remove the stones. Scoop a little of the pulp out from each and combine in a small bowl with the crushed biscuits, egg yolk, caster sugar, ground almonds and amaretto.

Spoon some of the mixture into each peach and place them, cut side up, in the dish. Sprinkle with the white wine and the extra sugar. Place a dot of butter on the top of each and bake for 20–25 minutes, or until golden.

PREPARATION TIME: 15 MINUTES   COOKING TIME: 25 MINUTES

ZUPPA INGLESE

500 ml (17 fl oz/2 cups) milk
1 vanilla bean, split lengthways
4 egg yolks
115 g (4 oz/½ cup) caster (superfine) sugar
2 tablespoons plain (all-purpose) flour
300 g (10½ oz) Madeira cake, cut into 1 cm (½ inch) slices
80 ml (2½ fl oz/⅓ cup) rum
30 g (1 oz) chocolate, grated or shaved
50 g (1¾ oz) flaked almonds, toasted

SERVES 6

Heat the milk and vanilla bean in a saucepan over low heat until bubbles appear around the edge of the pan.

Whisk the egg yolks, sugar and flour together in a bowl until thick and pale.

Discard the vanilla bean and whisk the warm milk slowly into the egg mixture, then blend well. Return to a clean saucepan and stir over medium heat until the custard boils and thickens. Allow to cool slightly.

Line the base of a 1.5 litre (52 fl oz/6-cup) serving dish with one-third of the cake slices and brush well with the rum combined with 1 tablespoon water. Spread one-third of the custard over the cake. Repeat this process, finishing with a layer of custard. Cover and refrigerate for 3 hours. Sprinkle with chocolate and almonds just before serving.

PREPARATION TIME: 25 MINUTES +   COOKING TIME: 5 MINUTES

MACERATED BERRIES WITH MASCARPONE

125 g (4¹/₂ oz) blackberries
125 g (4¹/₂ oz) raspberries
155 g (5¹/₂ oz) blueberries
125 g (4¹/₂ oz) loganberries or similar
1-2 tablespoons caster (superfine) sugar
2 oranges
2 tablespoons sugar
mascarpone cheese, lightly stirred,
to serve

SERVES 4–6

Combine all the berries in a bowl, sprinkle the caster sugar over the top and toss lightly. Cover and refrigerate.

Peel the oranges and cut the zest into long, thin strips. Bring a small saucepan of water to the boil and blanch the orange strips, then drain. Repeat this twice more to remove any bitterness from the zest.

Combine 80 ml (2¹/₂ fl oz/¹/₃ cup) water with the sugar in a small saucepan and stir over low heat until the sugar dissolves. Add the orange zest and simmer gently for 1-2 minutes, or until just tender. Cool.

Reserve 1 tablespoon of the orange strips and lightly mix the rest with the cooking syrup and berries.

To serve, spoon the berry mixture into goblets. Garnish with the mascarpone and reserved orange zest strips.

PREPARATION TIME: 20 MINUTES +   COOKING TIME: 10 MINUTES

ESPRESSO GRANITA

2 tablespoons caster (superfine) sugar
500 ml (17 fl oz/2 cups) hot espresso
coffee
lightly whipped cream, to serve

SERVES 6

Dissolve the sugar in the coffee and stir thoroughly until dissolved. Pour into a shallow metal container or tray and cool completely. Freeze for 30 minutes, then scrape with a fork to distribute the ice crystals evenly. Freeze again for 30 minutes.

Using a fork, scrape the granita into fine crystals and return to the freezer for 1 hour before serving. Spoon into glasses and top with a dollop of lightly whipped cream.

PREPARATION TIME: 10 MINUTES +   COOKING TIME: NIL

NOTE: Use a shallow tray and break the granita up when partially frozen. It is difficult to break up if made in a deep container.

SICILIAN CANNOLI

FILLING
500 g (1 lb 2 oz) ricotta cheese
1 teaspoon orange flower water
100 g (3¹/₂ oz/¹/₂ cup) cedro, diced
(see Notes)
60 g (2¹/₄ oz) bittersweet chocolate,
coarsely grated or chopped
1 tablespoon grated orange zest
60 g (2¹/₄ oz/¹/₂ cup) icing
(confectioners') sugar

300 g (10¹/₂ oz) plain (all-purpose) flour
1 tablespoon caster (superfine) sugar
1 teaspoon ground cinnamon
40 g (1¹/₂ oz) unsalted butter
60 ml (2 fl oz/¹/₄ cup) Marsala
vegetable oil, for deep-frying
icing (confectioners') sugar, to dust

MAKES 12

To make the filling, combine all the ingredients in a bowl and mix. Add 2 tablespoons water and mix well to form a dough. Cover with plastic wrap and refrigerate.

Combine the flour, sugar and cinnamon in a bowl, rub in the butter and add the Marsala. Mix until the dough comes together in a loose clump, then knead on a lightly floured surface for 4–5 minutes, or until smooth. Wrap in plastic wrap and refrigerate for at least 30 minutes.

Cut the dough in half and roll each portion on a lightly floured surface into a thin sheet about 5 mm (¹/₄ inch) thick. Cut each dough half into six 9 cm (3¹/₂ inch) squares. Place a metal tube (see Note) diagonally across the middle of each square. Fold the sides over the tube, moistening the overlap with water, then press together.

Heat the oil in a large deep frying pan to 180°C (350°F), or until a cube of bread dropped into the oil browns in 15 seconds. Drop one or two tubes at a time into the hot oil. Fry gently until golden brown and crisp. Remove from the oil, gently remove the moulds and drain on crumpled paper towels. When they are cool, fill a piping (icing) bag with the ricotta mixture and fill the shells. Dust with icing sugar and serve.

PREPARATION TIME: 30 MINUTES +   COOKING TIME: 5 MINUTES

NOTES: Cannoli tubes are available at kitchenware shops. You can also use 2 cm (³/₄ inch) diameter wooden dowels cut into 12 cm (4¹/₂ inch) lengths.

Cedro, also known as citron, is a citrus fruit with a very thick, knobbly skin. The skin is used to make candied peel.

RICE PUDDING

600 ml (21 fl oz) milk
250 ml (9 fl oz/1 cup) thick (double/heavy) cream
1 vanilla bean, split
50 g (1³/4 oz) caster (superfine) sugar
¹/4 teaspoon ground cinnamon
pinch freshly grated nutmeg
1 tablespoon grated orange zest
80 g (2³/4 oz/¹/2 cup) sultanas (golden raisins)
2 tablespoons brandy or sweet Marsala
110 g (3³/4 oz/¹/2 cup) risotto rice

SERVES 4

Put the milk, cream and vanilla bean in a heavy-based saucepan and bring just to the boil, then remove from the heat. Stir in the sugar, cinnamon, nutmeg and orange zest and set aside.

Soak the sultanas in the brandy. Meanwhile, add the rice to the infused milk and return to the heat. Bring to a simmer and stir slowly for about 35 minutes, or until the rice is creamy. Stir in the sultanas and remove the vanilla bean at the end. Serve warm or cold.

PREPARATION TIME: 10 MINUTES   COOKING TIME: 40 MINUTES

RICE PUDDING WITH LEMON THYME AND BALSAMIC STRAWBERRIES

500 g (1 lb 2 oz) strawberries, halved
2 tablespoons balsamic vinegar
80 g (2³/4 oz/¹/3 cup) caster (superfine) sugar
150 g (5¹/2 oz/³/4 cup) long-grain white rice
750 ml (26 fl oz/3 cups) milk
6 x 3 cm (1¹/4 inch) lemon thyme sprigs
80 g (2³/4 oz/¹/3 cup) sugar
3 egg yolks
1 egg

SERVES 6–8

Put the strawberries in a bowl with the vinegar. Sprinkle the caster sugar over the top and stir well. Set aside, turning occasionally.

Preheat the oven to 160°C (315°F/Gas 2–3). Lightly grease a 1.5 litre (52 fl oz/6-cup) ovenproof dish. Thoroughly rinse the rice and put it in a saucepan with 375 ml (13 fl oz/1¹/2 cups) water. Bring to the boil, cover and cook over low heat for 8–10 minutes. Remove from the heat and leave the pan with the lid on for 5 minutes, until the liquid is absorbed.

Heat the milk with the lemon thyme and sugar in a saucepan. When bubbles form at the edge, remove from the heat and set aside for 10 minutes. Strain. Beat the egg yolks and egg in a bowl, add the rice and gradually stir in the warm milk. Pour into the prepared dish. Place the dish in a baking dish and pour in enough warm water to come halfway up the side of the dish. Bake for 50–60 minutes, or until the pudding is just set. Remove from the oven and stand for 10 minutes. Serve warm or cold with the balsamic strawberries.

PREPARATION TIME: 20 MINUTES +   COOKING TIME: 1 HOUR 15 MINUTES

HONEY AND PINE NUT TART

PASTRY
250 g (9 oz/2 cups) plain (all-purpose) flour
1¹/₂ tablespoons icing (confectioners') sugar
115 g (4 oz) chilled unsalted butter, chopped
1 egg, lightly beaten

235 g (8¹/₂ oz/1¹/₂ cups) pine nuts
175 g (6 oz/¹/₂ cup) honey
115 g (4 oz) unsalted butter, extra, softened
115 g (4 oz/¹/₂ cup) caster (superfine) sugar
3 eggs, lightly beaten
¹/₄ teaspoon natural vanilla extract
1 tablespoon almond liqueur
1 teaspoon finely grated lemon zest
1 tablespoon lemon juice
icing (confectioners') sugar, to dust
crème fraîche or mascarpone, to serve

SERVES 6

Preheat the oven to 190°C (375°F/Gas 5) and place a baking tray on the middle shelf. Lightly grease a 23 cm (9 inch), 3.5 cm (1¹/₂ inch) deep loose-based tart tin.

To make the pastry, sift the flour and icing sugar into a large bowl and add the butter. Rub the butter into the flour with your fingertips until it resembles fine breadcrumbs. Make a well in the centre and add the egg and 2 tablespoons cold water. Mix with a flat-bladed knife, using a cutting action, until the mixture comes together in beads.

Gather the dough together and lift out onto a lightly floured work surface. Press together into a ball, roll out to a circle 3 mm (¹/₈ inch) thick and invert into the tin. Use a small ball of pastry to press the pastry into the tin, allowing any excess to hang over the sides. Roll a rolling pin over the tin, cutting off any excess pastry. Prick the base all over with a fork and chill for 15 minutes. Roll out the pastry scraps and cut out three leaves for decoration. Cover and refrigerate for 15 minutes.

Line the pastry with baking paper and fill with baking beads or uncooked rice. Bake on the heated tray for 10 minutes, then remove the tart tin, leaving the tray in the oven. Reduce the oven to 180°C (350°F/Gas 4).

To make the filling, spread the pine nuts on a baking tray and roast in the oven for 3 minutes, or until golden. Heat the honey in a small saucepan until runny, then allow to cool. Cream the butter and sugar in a bowl until smooth and pale. Gradually add the eggs, beating well after each addition. Mix in the honey, vanilla, liqueur, lemon zest and juice and a pinch of salt. Stir in the pine nuts, spoon into the pastry case and smooth the surface. Arrange the reserved pastry leaves in the centre.

Place the tin on the hot tray and bake for 40 minutes, or until golden and set. Cover the top with foil after 25 minutes. Serve warm or at room temperature, dusted with icing sugar. Serve with crème fraîche or mascarpone.

PREPARATION TIME: 25 MINUTES +   COOKING TIME: 1 HOUR

ALMOND SEMIFREDDO

310 ml (10³/4 fl oz/1¹/4 cups) pouring (whipping) cream
4 eggs, at room temperature, separated
85 g (3 oz/²/3 cup) icing (confectioners') sugar
60 ml (2 fl oz/¹/4 cup) amaretto
80 g (2³/4 oz/¹/2 cup) toasted almonds, chopped
8 amaretti biscuits, crushed
fresh fruit or extra amaretto, to serve

SERVES 8–10

Whip the cream until firm peaks form, then cover and refrigerate. Line a 10 x 21 cm (4 x 8¹/2 inch) loaf (bar) tin with plastic wrap so that it overhangs the two long sides.

Beat the egg yolks and icing sugar in a large bowl until pale and creamy. Whisk the egg whites in a separate bowl until firm peaks form. Stir the amaretto, almonds and amaretti biscuits into the egg yolk mixture, then carefully fold in the chilled cream and the egg whites until well combined. Carefully pour or spoon into the lined loaf tin and cover with the overhanging plastic. Freeze for 4 hours, or until frozen but not rock hard. Serve slices with fresh fruit or a sprinkling of amaretto.

PREPARATION TIME: 30 MINUTES +   COOKING TIME: NIL

NOTES: Semifreddo means semi frozen, so if you leave it in the freezer overnight, put it in the refrigerator for 30 minutes before serving.
    The semifreddo can also be frozen in individual moulds or serving dishes.

MARINATED FIGS WITH RASPBERRY SAUCE

6 figs, halved
310 ml (10³/4 fl oz/1¹/4 cups) dessert wine
1 cinnamon stick
1 tablespoon soft brown sugar
310 g (11 oz) raspberries, plus extra, to garnish
55 g (2¹/4 oz/¹/4 cup) caster (superfine) sugar
1 teaspoon lemon juice
110 g (3³/4 oz/¹/2 cup) mascarpone cheese

SERVES 4

Place the figs in a glass or ceramic bowl. Combine the wine, cinnamon and sugar in a small saucepan and warm over low heat. When the sugar has dissolved, pour over the figs. Cover and allow to stand for 2 hours.

Blend the raspberries and caster sugar in a food processor. Push through a sieve, then stir in the lemon juice.

Drain the figs. Strain and reserve the marinade. Grill (broil) the figs until golden. Pour a little raspberry sauce onto each dessert plate. Arrange three fig halves on each plate and drizzle with the marinade. Serve with the mascarpone.

PREPARATION TIME: 20 MINUTES +   COOKING TIME: 10 MINUTES

SICILIAN RICE FRITTERS

110 g (3³/4 oz/¹/2 cup) risotto rice
330 ml (11¹/4 fl oz/1¹/3 cups) milk
10 g (¹/4 oz) unsalted butter
1 tablespoon caster (superfine) sugar
1 vanilla bean, scraped
1 teaspoon dried yeast
2 tablespoons cedro, finely chopped
2 teaspoons grated lemon zest
vegetable oil, for deep-frying
plain (all-purpose) flour, for rolling
2 tablespoons fragrant honey

MAKES 8

Combine the rice, milk, butter, sugar, vanilla bean and scraped seeds, and a pinch of salt in a heavy-based saucepan. Bring to the boil over medium heat, then reduce the heat to very low. Cover and cook for 15–18 minutes, or until most of the liquid has been absorbed. Remove from the heat, cover and set aside.

Dissolve the yeast in 2 tablespoons tepid water and allow to stand for 5 minutes, or until frothy. If your yeast doesn't foam, it is dead and you will have to start again.

Discard the vanilla bean from the rice mixture. Add the yeast, cedro and lemon zest to the rice. Mix well, cover and allow to stand for 1 hour.

Fill a deep-fryer or heavy-based saucepan one-third full of oil and heat to 180°C (350°F), or until a spoonful of the batter dropped into the oil browns in 15 seconds.

Shape the rice into croquettes about 2.5 x 8 cm (1 x 3¹/4 inches) and roll them in flour. Deep-fry in batches for 5–6 minutes, or until golden brown on all sides. Remove with a slotted spoon and drain on crumpled paper towels. Drizzle with honey and serve immediately.

PREPARATION TIME: 20 MINUTES +   COOKING TIME: 25 MINUTES

MACERATED ORANGES

4 oranges
1 teaspoon grated lemon zest
55 g (2 oz/¼ cup) caster (superfine) sugar
1 tablespoon lemon juice
2 tablespoons Cointreau or Maraschino (optional)

SERVES 4

Cut a thin slice off the top and bottom of the oranges. Using a small sharp knife, slice off the skin and pith, removing as much pith as possible. Slice down the side of a segment between the flesh and the membrane. Repeat on the other side and lift the segment out. Do this over a bowl to catch the juice. Repeat with all the segments. Squeeze out any juice remaining in the membranes.

Place the segments on a shallow dish and sprinkle with the lemon zest, sugar and lemon juice. Toss carefully. Cover and refrigerate for at least 2 hours. Toss again. Serve chilled. Add Cointreau or Maraschino just before serving, if desired.

PREPARATION TIME: 10 MINUTES + COOKING TIME: NIL

RICOTTA POTS WITH RASPBERRIES

4 eggs, separated
115 g (4 oz/½ cup) caster (superfine) sugar
350 g (12 oz) ricotta cheese
35 g (1¼ oz/¼ cup) finely chopped pistachio nuts
1 teaspoon grated lemon zest
2 tablespoons lemon juice
1 tablespoon vanilla sugar (see Note)
200 g (7 oz) raspberries
icing (confectioners') sugar, to dust

SERVES 4

Preheat the oven to 180°C (350°F/Gas 4). Beat the egg yolks and sugar in a small bowl until thick and pale. Transfer to a large bowl and add the ricotta, pistachio nuts, lemon zest and juice and mix well.

In a separate bowl, whisk the egg whites to stiff peaks. Beat in the vanilla sugar, then gently fold into the ricotta mixture, until just combined.

Lightly grease four 250 ml (9 fl oz/1-cup) ramekins. Divide the raspberries among the dishes and spoon the ricotta filling over the top. Place on a baking tray and bake for 20–25 minutes, or until puffed and lightly browned. Serve immediately, dusted with a little icing sugar.

PREPARATION TIME: 20 MINUTES   COOKING TIME: 25 MINUTES

NOTE: You can buy vanilla sugar or make your own. Split a whole vanilla bean in half lengthways and place in a jar of caster sugar (about 1 kg/2 lb 4 oz). Leave for at least 4 days before using.'

RICE TART

PASTRY

155 g (5¹/₂ oz/1¹/₄ cups) plain
(all-purpose) flour
55 g (2¹/₄ oz/¹/₄ cup) caster
(superfine) sugar
125 g (4¹/₂ oz) cold unsalted butter,
cut into 1 cm (¹/₂ inch) cubes
2 egg yolks
1 teaspoon natural vanilla extract

FILLING

60 g (2¹/₄ oz/¹/₂ cup) raisins
2 tablespoons cognac or brandy
110 g (3³/₄ oz/¹/₂ cup) risotto rice
750 ml (26 fl oz/3 cups) pouring
(whipping) cream
1 vanilla bean, split
2 cinnamon sticks
6 egg yolks
180 g (6¹/₂ oz/³/₄ cup) caster
(superfine) sugar
50 g (1³/₄ oz/¹/₃ cup) pine nuts, toasted
1¹/₂ teaspoons finely grated lemon zest
lightly whipped cream, to serve

SERVES 8–10

To make the pastry, sift the flour into a bowl and add the sugar and a pinch of salt. Add the butter and toss to coat in the flour mix. Rub the butter into the flour with your fingertips for about 5 minutes, or until it resembles fine breadcrumbs, then make a well in the centre.

Mix the egg yolks, vanilla and 60 ml (2 fl oz/¹/₄ cup) cold water together, then pour into the well. Using a flat-bladed knife, cut into the mixture while you turn the bowl until it is well combined and comes together in small beads. If it still crumbles, add 1 more teaspoon of water.

Gather the dough together. Press into a ball. Flatten into a 2 cm (³/₄ inch) thick disc. Cover with plastic wrap and refrigerate for 30 minutes.

Roll the pastry out between two sheets of plastic wrap until it is 36 cm (14 inches) in diameter. Remove the top layer of baking paper and invert the pastry onto a 28 cm (11¹/₄ inch) fluted tart dish or tin with 4 cm (1¹/₂ inch) sides. Remove the final layer of paper and press the pastry into the dish, allowing any extra to hang over the sides, then trim the edges using a knife. Prick the base all over with a fork then refrigerate for 1 hour.

Preheat the oven to 180°C (350°F/Gas 4). Combine the raisins and cognac. Set aside to soak. Cook the rice in boiling water for 15 minutes, or until tender. Drain, rinse with cold water and leave to drain and cool. Place the cream, vanilla bean and cinnamon in a saucepan and bring almost to the boil over medium heat. Remove from the heat. Set aside to cool.

Remove the tart from the fridge, line with lightly crumpled baking paper and pour in some baking beads and spread evenly over the base. Bake for 15 minutes then remove the paper and beads and cook for a further 10–15 minutes, or until lightly golden all over. Remove from the oven and set aside to cool. Reduce the temperature to 150°C (300°F/Gas 2).

Beat the egg yolks and sugar together until thick. Strain the cream mixture and stir into the eggs. Combine the rice with the raisins, pine nuts and lemon zest. Spread the rice mixture over the base of the tart shell, then pour over the custard. Bake for 45 minutes, or until just set. Allow to cool. Serve with lightly whipped cream.

PREPARATION TIME: 25 MINUTES +   COOKING TIME: 1 HOUR 35 MINUTES

PANNA COTTA WITH RUBY SAUCE

750 ml (26 fl oz/3 cups) pouring (whipping) cream
3 teaspoons gelatine
1 vanilla bean
80 g (2³/₄ oz/¹/₃ cup) caster (superfine) sugar

RUBY SAUCE
230 g (8¹/₂ oz/1 cup) caster (superfine) sugar
1 cinnamon stick
125 g (4¹/₂ oz) fresh or frozen raspberries, plus extra, to serve
125 ml (4 fl oz/¹/₂ cup) red wine

SERVES 6

Lightly grease six 150 ml (5 fl oz) ramekins or moulds with flavourless oil. Place 60 ml (2 fl oz/¹/₄ cup) of the cream in a small bowl, sprinkle the gelatine in an even layer over the surface and leave to go spongy.

Put the remaining cream in a saucepan with the vanilla bean and sugar and heat gently while stirring. Remove from the heat. Whisk the gelatine into the cream mixture. Pour into the moulds and chill for 2 hours, or until set. Unmould by wiping a cloth dipped in hot water over the mould and upending it onto a plate.

While the panna cotta is chilling, make the ruby sauce. Stir the sugar with 250 ml (9 fl oz/1 cup) water in a saucepan over medium heat until the sugar has dissolved. Add the cinnamon stick and simmer for 5 minutes. Add the raspberries and wine and boil rapidly for 5 minutes. Remove the cinnamon stick and push the sauce through a sieve. Discard the seeds. Cool, then chill before serving with the panna cotta. Serve with raspberries.

PREPARATION TIME: 20 MINUTES +   COOKING TIME: 20 MINUTES

BELLINI SORBET

460 g (1 lb/2 cups) caster (superfine) sugar
5 large peaches
185 ml (6 fl oz/³/₄ cup) Champagne
2 egg whites, lightly beaten

SERVES 6

Combine the sugar with 1 litre (35 fl oz/4 cups) water in a large saucepan and stir over low heat until the sugar has dissolved. Bring to the boil, add the peaches and simmer for 20 minutes. Remove the peaches and cool. Reserve 250 ml (9 fl oz/1 cup) of the poaching liquid.

Peel the peaches, remove the stones and cut the flesh into chunks. Chop in a food processor until smooth, add the reserved liquid and the Champagne and process briefly until combined. Pour into a shallow metal tray and freeze for about 6 hours, until just firm. Transfer to a large bowl and beat until smooth using electric beaters. Refreeze and repeat this step twice more, adding the egg white on the final beating. Place in a storage container, cover the surface with baking paper and freeze until firm. Serve the sorbet in scoops.

PREPARATION TIME: 20 MINUTES +   COOKING TIME: 25 MINUTES

Panna cotta with ruby sauce

SWEET CHEESE IN LEMON PASTA

PASTA
250 g (9 oz/2 cups) plain (all-purpose) flour
1/2 teaspoon salt
1 teaspoon caster (superfine) sugar
grated zest of 2 lemons
2 tablespoons lemon juice
2 eggs, lightly beaten

FILLING
1 tablespoon currants
1 tablespoon brandy
600 g (1 lb 5 oz) ricotta cheese
40 g (1¹/₂ oz/¹/₃ cup) icing (confectioners') sugar, plus extra, to dust
³/₄ teaspoon grated lemon zest
³/₄ teaspoon natural vanilla extract
30 g (1 oz/¹/₃ cup) flaked almonds, toasted

beaten egg, for glazing
vegetable oil, for frying
250 ml (9 fl oz/1 cup) pouring (whipping) cream, flavoured with brandy, to taste
mint leaves, to garnish
thin strips of lemon zest, to garnish, (optional)

SERVES 4–6

To make the pasta, pile the combined flour, salt, sugar and lemon zest on a work surface and make a well in the centre. Add 1–2 tablespoons water, the lemon juice and egg and gradually blend them into the flour, using a fork. When a loosely combined dough forms, use your hands and begin kneading. Incorporate a little extra flour if the dough feels moist. Knead for 5–8 minutes, or until smooth and elastic. Cover with plastic wrap and set aside for 15 minutes.

Soak the currants in the brandy in a bowl. In a larger bowl, combine the ricotta cheese, icing sugar, lemon zest and vanilla. Set aside.

Divide the dough into eight equal portions. Roll each out to a thin sheet about 18 cm (7 inches) square. Cover each as it is completed.

Trim each pasta sheet into a neat square. Working with a few at a time, brush around the edges with beaten egg. Add the currants and toasted almonds to the ricotta filling, then put one-eighth of the filling in the middle of each square of dough. Fold the edges over to completely enclose the filling. Press the edges down to seal.

Heat oil in a pan to 1–2 cm (about ¹/₂ inch) depth. Drop a piece of scrap pasta in to check that it turns golden without burning. Fry the parcels, two or three at a time, until golden. Remove with a slotted spoon, drain on paper towels and keep warm. Serve with brandy cream, sprinkled with icing sugar and garnished with mint leaves and lemon zest.

PREPARATION TIME: 1 HOUR +   COOKING TIME: 25 MINUTES

ZUCCOTTO

1 ready-made sponge cake
80 ml (2$\frac{1}{2}$ fl oz/$\frac{1}{3}$ cup) Kirsch
60 ml (2 fl oz/$\frac{1}{4}$ cup) Cointreau
80 ml (2$\frac{1}{2}$ fl oz/$\frac{1}{3}$ cup) rum, Cognac,
Grand Marnier or Maraschino
500 ml (17 fl oz/2 cups) pouring
(whipping) cream
90 g (3$\frac{1}{4}$ oz) dark roasted almond
chocolate, chopped
175 g (6 oz) finely chopped mixed
glacé fruit
100 g (3$\frac{1}{2}$ oz) dark chocolate, melted
70 g (2$\frac{1}{2}$ oz) hazelnuts, roasted
and chopped
unsweetened cocoa powder and icing
(confectioners') sugar, to decorate

SERVES 6–8

Line a 1.5 litre (52 fl oz/6-cup) pudding basin (mould) with damp muslin (cheesecloth). Cut the cake into curved pieces with a knife (you will need about 12 pieces). Work with one strip of cake at a time, brushing it with the combined liqueurs and arranging the pieces closely in the basin. Put the thin ends in the centre so the slices cover the base and side of the basin. Brush with the remaining liqueur to soak the cake. Chill.

Beat the cream until stiff peaks form, then divide in half. Fold the almond chocolate and glacé fruit into one half and spread evenly over the cake in the basin, leaving a space in the centre.

Fold the cooled melted chocolate and hazelnuts into the remaining cream and spoon into the centre cavity, packing it in firmly. Smooth the surface, cover and chill for 8 hours to allow the cream to firm slightly. Turn out onto a plate and dust with cocoa powder and icing sugar.

PREPARATION TIME: 1 HOUR +   COOKING TIME: NIL

AMARETTI

1 tablespoon plain (all-purpose) flour
1 tablespoon cornflour (cornstarch)
1 teaspoon ground cinnamon
145 g (5 oz/$\frac{2}{3}$ cup) caster (superfine)
sugar
1 teaspoon grated lemon zest
100 g (3$\frac{1}{2}$ oz/1 cup) ground almonds
2 egg whites
30 g (1 oz/$\frac{1}{4}$ cup) icing (confectioners')
sugar

MAKES 40

Line two baking trays with baking paper. Sift the plain flour, cornflour, cinnamon and half the caster sugar into a large bowl. Add the lemon zest and ground almonds.

Place the egg whites in a small dry bowl. Using electric beaters, beat the egg whites until soft peaks form. Add the remaining caster sugar gradually, beating constantly until the mixture is thick and glossy. Using a metal spoon, fold the egg white into the dry ingredients. Stir until the ingredients are just combined and the mixture forms a soft dough.

Roll two level teaspoons of mixture at a time into a ball. Arrange on the tray, allowing room for spreading. Set the tray aside for 1 hour before baking.

Heat the oven to 180°C (350°F/Gas 4). Sift the icing sugar over the biscuits. Bake for 15–20 minutes, or until crisp and lightly browned. Transfer to a wire rack to cool.

PREPARATION TIME: 15 MINUTES +   COOKING TIME: 20 MINUTES

ICE CREAM CASSATA

FIRST LAYER
2 eggs, separated

40 g (1½ oz/⅓ cup) icing (confectioners') sugar

185 ml (6 fl oz/¾ cup) pouring (whipping) cream

50 g (1¾ oz) flaked almonds, toasted

SECOND LAYER
130 g (4¾ oz) dark chocolate, chopped

1 tablespoon dark unsweetened cocoa powder

2 eggs, separated

40 g (1½ oz/⅓ cup) icing (confectioners') sugar

185 ml (6 fl oz/¾ cup) pouring (whipping) cream

THIRD LAYER
2 eggs, separated

30 g (1 oz/¼ cup) icing (confectioners') sugar

60 ml (2 fl oz/¼ cup) pouring (whipping) cream

125 g (4½ oz/½ cup) ricotta cheese

250 g (9 oz) glacé fruit (pineapple, apricot, cherries, fig and peach), finely chopped

1 teaspoon natural vanilla extract

SERVES 10

Line the base and sides of a deep 20 cm (8 inch) square tin with foil.

To make the first layer, beat the egg whites with electric beaters until soft peaks form. Add the icing sugar gradually, beating well after each addition. In a separate bowl, beat the cream until firm peaks form. Using a metal spoon, fold the yolks and beaten egg whites into the cream. Stir in the almonds. Spoon into the tin and smooth the surface. Tap the tin gently on the bench to level the surface, then freeze for 30-60 minutes, or until firm.

To make the second layer, melt the chocolate by stirring in a heatproof bowl over a saucepan of steaming water, off the heat. Make sure the base of the bowl does not touch the water. Stir in the cocoa until smooth. Cool slightly, then proceed as for step 1, beating the egg whites and icing sugar and then the cream. Using a metal spoon, fold the chocolate into the cream. Fold in the yolks and beaten egg whites and stir until smooth. Spoon over the frozen first layer. Tap the tin on the bench to smooth the surface. Freeze for 30-60 minutes, or until firm.

To make the third layer, proceed as for the first layer, beating the egg whites with the icing sugar and then the cream. Stir the ricotta into the cream. With a metal spoon, fold the yolks and egg white into the cream, then stir in the fruit and vanilla extract. Spoon over the chocolate layer, cover the surface with baking paper, then freeze overnight. Slice to serve.

PREPARATION TIME: 50 MINUTES +   COOKING TIME: NIL

BISCOTTI

250 g (9 oz/2 cups) plain (all-purpose)
flour
1 teaspoon baking powder
230 g (8 oz/1 cup) caster (superfine)
sugar
3 eggs
1 egg yolk
1 teaspoon natural vanilla extract
1 teaspoon grated orange zest
110 g (3³/₄ oz/³/₄ cup) pistachio nuts

MAKES 45

Preheat the oven to 180°C (350°F/Gas 4). Line two baking trays with baking paper and lightly dust with flour.

Sift the flour and baking powder into a large bowl. Add the sugar and mix well. Make a well in the centre and add two whole eggs, the egg yolk, vanilla extract and orange zest. Using a large metal spoon, stir until just combined. Mix in the pistachios. Knead for 2–3 minutes on a floured surface. The dough will be stiff at first. Sprinkle a little water onto the dough. Divide the mixture into two portions and roll each into a log about 25 cm (10 inches) long and 8 cm (3¹/₄ inches) wide. Slightly flatten the tops.

Place the logs on the trays, allowing room for spreading. Beat the remaining egg and brush over the logs to glaze. Bake for 35 minutes, then remove from the oven.

Reduce the oven to 150°C (300°F/Gas 2). Allow the logs to cool slightly and cut each into 5 mm (¹/₄ inch) slices. Place, flat side down, on the trays and bake for 8 minutes. Turn the biscuits over and cook for a further 8 minutes, or until slightly coloured and crisp and dry. Transfer to a wire rack to cool completely. Store in an airtight container.

PREPARATION TIME: 25 MINUTES   COOKING TIME: 50 MINUTES

LEMON GRANITA

310 ml (10³/₄ fl oz/1¹/₄ cups) lemon juice
1 tablespoon grated lemon zest
200 g (7 oz) caster (superfine) sugar

SERVES 4–6

Place the lemon juice, zest and sugar in a small saucepan and stir over low heat for 5 minutes, or until the sugar is dissolved. Allow to cool.

Add 500 ml (17 fl oz/2 cups) water to the lemon mixture and mix well. Pour into a shallow 20 x 30 cm (8 x 12 inch) metal container or tray and cool completely. Freeze for 30 minutes, then scrape with a fork to distribute the ice crystals evenly. Return to the freezer for 30 minutes.

Using a fork, scrape the granita into fine crystals and return to the freezer for 1 hour before serving. Spoon into chilled glasses and serve immediately.

PREPARATION TIME: 15 MINUTES +   COOKING TIME: 5 MINUTES

INDEX

INDEX